Complete Prayers for Young People

Professor Barclay was a distinguished scholar, an exceptionally gifted preacher and a regular broadcaster. His writings for the *British Weekly* were very popular and for twenty years from 1950 a full page every week was given to them. From 1963 until 1974 he was Professor of Divinity and Biblical Criticism at Glasgow University. He was a Member of the Advisory Committee working on the New English Bible and also a Member of the Apocrypha Panel of Translators.

In 1975 he was appointed a Visiting Professor at the University of Strathclyde for a period of three years where he lectured on Ethics, and in the same year – jointly with the Rev. Professor James Stewart – he received the 1975 Citation from the American theological organization The Upper Room; the first time it had been awarded outside America. His extremely popular *Bible Study Notes* using his own translation of the New Testament have achieved a world-wide sale. Professor Barclay died in January 1978.

COMPLETE PRAYERS FOR YOUNG PEOPLE

PRAYERS FOR YOUNG PEOPLE
MORE PRAYERS FOR YOUNG PEOPLE

William Barclay

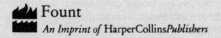

Fount
An Imprint of HarperCollinsPublishers

Fount Paperbacks is an Imprint of
HarperCollins*Religious*
Part of HarperCollins*Publishers*
77–85 Fulham Palace Road, London W6 8JB

Previously published as:
Prayers for Young People; first published in Great Britain in
1963 by William Collins Sons & Co. Ltd; Issued in Fontana
Books 1966; Reprinted by Fount Paperbacks 1977.
Copyright © 1963 by William Barclay
More Prayers for Young People; first published in Great Britain in
1977 by Fount Paperbacks.
Copyright © 1977 by William Barclay

This edition first published in Great Britain in 1996 by
Fount Paperbacks

  3 5 7 9 10 8 6 4 2

This Edition Copyright © 1996 by William Barclay

A catalogue record for this book is
available from the British Library

000 62 80293

Printed and bound in Great Britain by
Caledonian International Book Manufacturing Ltd, Glasgow

Contents

Prayers for Young People

For Fiona

Introduction

You and Your Prayers

Prayer is like any other great and valuable gift or possession – we will never get the best and the most from it, unless
we learn to use it aright. This means that there are certain
things which we must always bear in mind when we pray.

    i.   The very first thing that we must remember is
that God wants us to pray to him. There are times when
people make it quite clear that we are a nuisance to them,
and when quite clearly they cannot be bothered with us.
No one is ever a nuisance to God. Once when Jesus talked
to God, he used a word to address God which to us is a
foreign word. He called God, 'Abba, Father' (Mark 14:36).
Afterwards Paul said that this word Abba is the word that
any Christian can use when he talks to God (Romans
8:15). It is just not possible to translate this word Abba
into English. It was the word which a young child used in
Palestine in the time of Jesus when he talked to his father,
just as to this day Arab boys and girls call their father *jaba*.
It is really the Eastern word for Daddy. This means that we
can talk to God just as easily and just as simply as we talk
to our own father in our own home.

    Once someone asked a wise man how to set about
praying. The wise man said: 'Just take a chair and put it

opposite you, and think to yourself that God is sitting on that chair, and just talk to him in the way that you would talk to your closest friend.'

Prayer should not be unnatural and difficult; it should be as natural and as easy as talking to the person you know and love best of all.

In prayer we do not need any special words or any special language. We do not need to say 'thou' and 'thee'. That is the way the Bible has it, because that is the way in which people used ordinarily to talk long ago. We can use to God the same kind of language as we use every day. We do not need to be in any special place to pray. We can pray anywhere. Of course, it is easier to pray in some places than it is in others. In a church or in a great cathedral we cannot help having a feeling of reverence. But God is just as near us in a room in our own home, on the street, in a classroom, on a playing field, on a hilltop, as he is in any church or in any cathedral. We do not need to be in any special position to pray to God. We can pray walking along the road, sitting in a chair, standing on a moor or by the seashore, even lying in bed, just as well as we can pray kneeling. When we pray, all we have got to do is just to speak to God as we speak to our best friend.

ii.   When we pray we have to remember that we do not need to squeeze things out of God, as if he had to be persuaded into giving them to us. God wants to give us his good gifts even more than we want to ask him for them. Sometimes when we want something from a human person, we have to pester him into giving it to us; we have to break down his resistance. But God is not like that. He is more eager to give than we are to ask.

iii.   Of course, that does not mean that, if we want something, we have only to ask for it. It is very important to remember that God knows what is good for us far better than we know ourselves; and there are times when we pray for things which in the end would not be for our good. When we were very young we often wanted to do things like playing with matches; or we often wanted far more sweets or fruit than was good for us; or we wanted to do something which more experienced people knew could only lead to trouble. When that kind of thing happened, those who loved us had to refuse to give us what we wanted. Sometimes God has to do that. It is not that God does not answer our prayers; it is that God answers them, not in our way, but in his.

There is a problem here. If God knows everything, if God knows what is good for us better than we know ourselves, why bother to pray at all? If God knows it all, what need is there for us to speak to him? We talk about God knowing our secret thoughts; if we go to Church at all, we must have heard the prayer which begins: 'Almighty God, unto whom all hearts be open, all desires known, and from whom no secrets are hid'; if this is so, what is the sense in praying to one who knows what we want to pray for before we pray for it?

This is something about which we must think, for we certainly will not ever really pray, if we think in our heart of hearts that prayer is really a waste of time. Let us think about this in relation to the five different kinds of prayer.

There is the prayer which we call *invocation*. Invocation literally means a calling in. In the prayer of invocation we ask for God's presence with us, or, to put it better, because God is always with us, we ask God to make us aware that he is with us. Now, one of the great stories of Jesus after his resurrection tells how he met in with two people who were on the road from Jerusalem to Emmaus. They did not recognize him, but they were thrilled and fascinated by the things which he told them. They came near to the village and to the house where these two people lived. And then it says of Jesus: 'He made as though he would have gone further.' But they begged him to come into their house and visit them, and so he did (Luke 24:28, 29). There is about God and Jesus what we can only call a very wonderful courtesy. We cannot go into someone else's house without an invitation. It would be very impolite and very discourteous to burst in all uninvited; we wait until we are asked. God is like that. God wants to come into our life; he wants to meet us; but he waits until we ask him to come in to us. Of course, God shows us in all kinds of ways that he wants us to know him and to love him and to talk to him; but, like a courteous guest, he waits until we invite him in just as Jesus did on the road to Emmaus long ago. That is the first reason why we must speak to him, although he knows it all already.

There is the prayer which we call *confession*. Confession means telling God about the wrong things that we have done, saying that we are sorry for them, and asking him to forgive us for them. We know what happens at home. We do something wrong, and then we regret it. We know quite well that our parents really know that we are sorry, and we know quite well that they will forgive us. But between us and them there is a kind of invisible barrier, there is the feeling that something is wrong, there is a kind of atmosphere of unhappiness and strangeness, until we go to them and say: 'I'm sorry I was bad; I'll try not to do it again.' And immediately we have gone to them and said it, things are all right again. It is just the same with us and God. We know that nothing that we can do will stop God loving us; we know that he is always willing to forgive us; but things are not right between us and him until we go to him and say that we are sorry for what we have done.

There is the prayer which we call *thanksgiving*. Thanksgiving means thanking God for all the good gifts which he has given to us. One of the great dangers of life is that we should take things for granted just because they come to us regularly and every day. And it is never enough just to feel grateful to those who are kind to us; we must sometimes express our gratitude in words. A great many people have had an experience like this. They have known when they were young that their parents were very good and very kind to them, but they never said thank you and never said how grateful they were. Then the day came when their parents died, and when they looked back, they were forced to say to themselves: 'I wish I had told my father and mother how grateful I was for all that they did for me.' It is only courteous and polite to say thanks when people are kind to us. It is just the same with God. It is an ugly thing to take everything as a matter of course and never to say a word of thanks.

There is the prayer which we call *petition*. Petition means asking God for the things which we know we need, not only the material things, but the qualities of mind and heart and character which will enable us to live well and to make something out of life. But, if God knows what we need even better than we do, and if God knows what is good for us better than we know ourselves, why ask him for anything? It often happens in life that an older and a wiser person knows very well that something would be good for a younger person; but he does not know whether the younger person would accept it, if he offered it, and sometimes he even knows that the younger person would refuse to accept it. Often God cannot give us the things we need until we are prepared to consent to take them; and petition means asking God to give us the things which he knows we need, and telling him that we are ready now to take them. In fact, the best kind of petition is to tell God what we want, and then to say to him: 'Lord, give me not what I want, but what you know I need. Your will be done.' Often a teacher knows that a pupil would make a first-class scholar, but he cannot give the extra teaching and the extra work and the extra study, unless he or she will accept them. Often a trainer knows that a pupil would make a first-class athlete, but he cannot give the extra training and discipline until he or she is willing to accept them. God knows what is best for us, but God cannot give it to us, until we tell him that we are ready to take it. That is why we must tell God that we are ready and willing to accept his gifts.

The last kind of prayer is the prayer which we call *intercession*. Intercession means praying for other people. It is very natural to pray for people when we love them and when we want the best for them. All men and women and boys and girls are children of God. If you want really to please a parent, and really to make a parent happy, then the surest way to do it is to do something for the parent's son or daughter. And it pleases God most of all when he knows that we love and care for others who are his children. That is why it brings special pleasure to God when we pray for others.

When we come to think of it, we can see quite clearly that, although God does know it all already, there is every reason for telling him about it in our prayers.

iv.   There is another thing which we must remember about prayer, and it is one of the most important things of all. We must never look on prayer as the easy way out, as the way to get things done without any effort and trouble and labour on our part. God will never do for us what we can do for ourselves, and, when we pray, we must immediately do all we can to make our own prayers come true. It would be no good at all to pray to God to make us good at our lessons and successful in our examinations, unless we work and study as hard as we can. It would be quite useless to pray to God to make us good at athletics, unless we train as strenuously as we can. If we are ill, it would be no good to pray to God to make us well again, unless we obey the doctor, observe the diet that is set down for us, and take the medicine which is prescribed for us. It would, for instance, be quite useless for a person with a stomach ulcer to pray to God for health, and then to continue living on a diet of fried food. Prayer is not God doing things for us; prayer is God helping us to do things for ourselves.

Someone has said that God has four answers to prayer. Sometimes he says, Yes. Sometimes he says, No. Sometimes he says, Wait. Most of all he says, If. He says: 'I will help you, *if* you will do everything you can to help yourself.'

It is the same when we pray for other people. It is no good asking God to help the poor people, or to cheer the lonely people, unless we are prepared to give something to help those who are poor, and to visit those who are lonely.

Prayer is not an excuse for being lazy and for pushing all the work off on to God; prayer is a way to finding the strength and ability to do things along with God that we could never have done by ourselves.

v. There is another way of putting this. Prayer is not usually escape from things; prayer is the way to find strength to bear and to overcome things. Prayer will not cure a condition, for instance, which requires an operation to make us well again; but prayer will make us able to be cheerful and calm so that we will get well all the sooner. Suppose we plan to do something on a certain day, and suppose we want the sun to shine, it is no good praying that it will not rain. Whether it rains or not depends on the natural laws on which this world is founded. What we can and ought to do is to pray that, hail, rain or shine, we will be able to enjoy ourselves. It is no good praying that we should win a race or a game;

what we can do is to pray that, win or lose, we should play fair, and that we should take victory or defeat in the right spirit. Prayer does not usually stop things happening; it enables us to bear them and to conquer them when they do happen. Prayer is not a way of running away from things; it is a way of meeting them and beating them.

vi.   There is one more thing left to say. Up to this point we have been thinking of prayer as if it were always we who were talking to God; but prayer is not only talking to God; prayer is just as much listening to God. Prayer is not only us telling God what we want; it is God telling us what he wants. It is not only us saying to God: 'Lord, I want you to do this for me'; it is us saying to God: 'Lord, what do you want me to do?' That must mean that in all our prayers there must be a time when we stop speaking and when we listen in silence for what God wants to say to us. In prayer we must never be so busy talking that we never listen, and we must never speak so much that we give God no chance to speak. Remember in prayer always to have a silence when we listen to God.

There are very many people who only pray when they are in trouble and when things go wrong. But it is a poor kind of person who only goes to visit a friend when he wants something out of him. We ought to pray every day in life, for we need God all the time. We ought to pray before we go out in the morning. Maybe we will not have much time in the morning but we can at least pray the prayer that old Sir Jacob Astley prayed before the Battle of Edgehill: 'O Lord, thou knowest how busy I must be this day; if I forget thee, do not thou forget me.' And we ought always to pray before we go to sleep at night. It will make a difference if we begin and continue and end every day with God.

This book is meant to help you to pray. There is in it a morning and evening prayer for each week for a year.

Sometimes people do not pray because they do not really know what to say and how to put it. This book is meant to help you every morning and every evening to have a minute or two with God. But I hope that this book will be only a start for you, and that very soon the day will come when you will not need this book to help you to pray any more, but when you can talk to God, not in the words of this book, but in your own words, as easily as you talk to your best friend.

Daily Prayers

First Month: First Week

MORNING

O God, my Father, thank you for last night's sleep and
thank you for today.

Help me to waste none of today's hours and to miss none
of today's opportunities.

Help me all through today always to obey my conscience
and always to do what I know is right, so that I may
do nothing for which I would be sorry and ashamed
at the end of the day.

Help me so to live today that at the end of the day I may
be tired but happy, with nothing to regret.

This I ask for Jesus' sake. Amen.

EVENING

Forgive me, O God, for anyone whom I have hurt, or
failed, or disappointed today, and for any wrong thing
I have said or done today.

Thank you for all the new things I have learned today
and for all the things I have enjoyed today.

Give me a good night's sleep tonight, and grant that
tomorrow morning I may waken refreshed for work
and for play.

This I ask for Jesus' sake. Amen.

First Month: Second Week

MORNING

Make me all through today, O God,
> Obedient to my parents;
> Respectful to my teachers;
> Diligent in my work;
> Fair in my games;
> Clean in my pleasure;
> Kind to those whom I can help;
> True to my friends;
> And loyal to you.

This I ask for Jesus' sake. Amen.

EVENING

O God, bless those who are not so fortunate as I am.

Bless those whose homes are unhappy and whose parents are unkind.

Bless those who are ill. Specially bless those who are away from home in hospitals and in infirmaries and who are feeling everything very strange and who are a little afraid.

Bless those who are poor and hungry and cold.

Grant that in my happiness I may not forget the needs of others.

This I ask for Jesus' sake. Amen.

First Month: Third Week

MORNING

O God, thank you for making me as I am.
Thank you for health and strength;
> For eyes to see;
> For ears to hear;
> For hands to work;
> For feet to walk and run;
> For a mind to think;
> For a memory to remember;
> For a heart to love.

Thank you for
> Parents who are kind to me;
> Friends who are true to me;
> Teachers who are patient with me.

Thank you for this wonderful life. Help me to try to
deserve all your gifts a little more.
This I ask for Jesus' sake. Amen.

EVENING

Thank you, O God, for everything that has happened
today, and thank you for bringing me safely to the
end of today.
Forgive me for anything I said or did today for which now
I am ashamed.
Forgive me,
> If I have worried my parents;
> If I have disappointed my friends;
> If I have caused trouble to my teachers;
> If I have let myself down.

Tomorrow is another day. Please help me to do better in it.
This I ask for Jesus' sake. Amen.

First Month: Fourth Week

MORNING

O God, help me to cure my faults.
Keep me from being
> Cheeky in my conversation;
> Sulky when I get a row which I deserve;
> Lazy at my lessons;
> Disobliging at home;
> Too conceited when I do well;
> Too discouraged when I fail.

Help me to walk looking to Jesus, and always to try to be more like him.
This I ask for his sake. Amen.

EVENING

Thank you, O God, for all the people with whom I have learned lessons, played games, and walked and talked today.

Thank you for all the people who have been kind to me today:
> For those whose work and whose love give me the things I need, the food I eat, the clothes I wear, the comfort I enjoy;
> For those who have taught me the things which I must know, if I am to do an adult's job in the world when I grow up;
> For those who are a fine example to me of how I ought to live;
> For friends without whom life could never be the same.

Thank you most of all for Jesus, my Master, my Example, my Friend.
Help me to sleep well tonight and to live well tomorrow.
This I ask for Jesus' sake. Amen.

First Month: Fifth Week

MORNING

O Lord Jesus, be with me all through today to help me
to live as I ought to live.

Be with me at my lessons,

so that I may never give up any task, no matter how
hard and difficult it is, until I have mastered it, and so
that I will not allow anything to beat me.

Be with me at my games,

so that, whether I win or lose, I may play fair, and so
that if I win I may not boast, and if I lose I may not
make excuses.

Be with me in my pleasure,

so that I may never find pleasure in anything that I
would afterwards regret, or in anything that I would
not like you or my parents to see me do.

Be with me in my home,

so that I may be kind and considerate, and that I may
try to make the work of others easier and not harder.

Be with me in the streets,

so that I may be a credit to my school and to my
uniform and to those who love me and to myself.

Help me to be the kind of person you want me to be.

This I ask for your love's sake. Amen.

EVENING

Forgive me, O God,

> If today there has been on my lips any word that was bad or untrue;
>
> If today there has been in my mind any thought that was envious or jealous or impure;
>
> If today I have listened to things which I should have refused to listen to;
>
> If today at any time I have been ashamed to show that I belong to you.

Help me to remember that you are always with me, so that I will always speak the truth, and do the right, and be afraid of nothing.

This I ask for Jesus' sake. Amen.

Second Month: First Week

MORNING

O God, all through today help me,

      Not to lose my temper even when people and things annoy me;

      Not to lose my patience even when things do not come out right the first time;

      Not to lose my hope when things are difficult and when learning is hard;

      Not to lose my goodness and my honour, even when I am tempted to take the wrong way.

Help me so to live today that I will have nothing to be sorry for when I go to bed again at night.

Hear this my prayer for Jesus' sake. Amen.

EVENING

O God, forgive me for anything that I have done today which I would not want my parents to know about and which I would not want you to see.

Forgive me for anything in today which I could have done very much better than I did it.

Forgive me for wasting my time, and for spending my time on the wrong things.

Forgive me for everything for which I am sorry now; and help me to sleep well tonight, and to do better tomorrow.

This I ask for Jesus' sake. Amen.

Second Month: Second Week

MORNING

Help me today, O God,

At school to concentrate on my work, and not to let my thoughts wander;

At games to play hard and to play fair;

At home to do my share in the work without grumbling and without having to be asked twice;

In my leisure time to enjoy myself in such a way that I will do good to myself and no harm to others.

Help me to make this a happy day for myself and for all whom I meet.

This I ask for Jesus' sake. Amen.

EVENING

O God, bless those who have to work while I sleep:

Those who work on the night shift in the works and factories and the shipyards and the mines;

Those who go on journeys on the roads and the railways, by sea and in the air, to bring us our letters, our newspapers, our food in the morning;

Police and watchmen who through the night protect the public peace and safety;

Doctors and nurses and all who through the night must care for those who are ill and in pain.

Help me to remember all those whose work keeps the world and its affairs going, while I sleep.

I know that you never slumber or sleep, and that your care for me and your watch over me are unsleeping and unceasing. Help me to sleep without fear, and to waken refreshed tomorrow.

This I ask for the sake of Jesus, my Lord. Amen.

Second Month: Third Week

MORNING

O God, all through today keep me

From girning and sulking when I do not get my
own way;

From being envious and jealous of others who
have what I have not got;

From doing things with a grumble and a grudge
when I am asked to help;

From making a nuisance of myself by being
obstinate and bad-tempered and disobliging.

All through today help me to make the best of everything
that happens, and to do with all my might whatever
my hand finds to do.

This I ask through Jesus Christ my Lord. Amen.

EVENING

O God, bless the people to whom I owe so much and
without whom my life could never be the same.

Bless my father and mother, and help me to try to show
them that I do love them and that I am grateful to
them.

Bless my brothers and sisters, and don't let there be any
fights and squabbles in this family.

Bless my friends, and keep me true to them and them
true to me.

Bless those who teach me, and help me to be a credit to
them.

Bless me. Forgive me for anything wrong I did or said
or thought today, and help me to do better tomorrow.

This I ask for Jesus' sake. Amen.

Second Month: Fourth Week

MORNING AT EXAMINATION TIME

O God, help me at my examination today to remember
the things which I have learned and studied.

Help me to remember well and to think clearly.

Help me not to be so nervous and excited that I will not
do myself justice, and keep me calm and clear-headed.

Help me to try my hardest and to do my best.

This I ask for your love's sake. Amen.

EVENING

O God, I know quite well that I bring most of my troubles
on myself.

I leave things until the last minute, and then I have
to do them in far too big a hurry to do them
properly, and so I often come to school with
lessons half-learned and work half-done.

I don't spend all the time I ought to spend in work
and in study, although I always mean to.

I get angry and impatient far too easily, and the
result is that I upset myself and everyone else.

I do things without thinking first, and then I am
sorry I did them.

I hurt the people I love most of all, and then – too
late – I am sorry for what I said or did.

It is not that I don't know what is right. I do know – but
the trouble is that I mean to do it and then don't do
it. I need your help to strengthen me and to change
me.

Please help me to do what I cannot do and to be what I
cannot be by myself.

This I ask for your love's sake. Amen.

Second Month: Fifth Week

MORNING

Today, O God, make me

> Brave enough to face the things of which I am afraid;
>
> Strong enough to overcome the temptations which try to make me do the wrong thing and not to do the right thing;
>
> Persevering enough to finish every task that is given me to do;
>
> Kind enough always to be ready to help others;
>
> Obedient enough to obey your voice whenever you speak to me through my conscience.

Help me

> To live in purity;
>
> To speak in truth;
>
> To act in love
>
> > All through today.

This I ask for Jesus' sake. Amen.

EVENING

O God, thank you for all the things and the people which
make such a difference to my life.

Thank you for

> My parents and for all that they give me and all
> that they do for me;
>
> My home and for all the happiness and the
> comfort which are always waiting there for
> me;
>
> My friends in whose company I am happy;
>
> My school and for everything I learn there to
> make me able some day to earn my own
> living and to live my own life;
>
> Jesus to be my Master, my Example, and my best
> and truest Friend.

Help me to try to deserve a little better all the wonderful
things which life and you have given to me.

This I ask for your love's sake. Amen.

Third Month: First Week

O God, help me to use today as you would wish me to use it.

Don't let me waste my time today. Help me always to know what I ought to be doing, and to do it.

Don't let me miss my opportunities today – opportunities to learn something new, opportunities to help someone in difficulty, opportunities to show those who love me that I love them, opportunities to make myself a little better and a little wiser than I am.

Don't let me quarrel with anyone today; no matter what happens, help me to keep my temper.

Don't let me let myself down today, and don't let me hurt or disappoint those who love me.

All through today don't let me forget Jesus, so that all through today I may try to make everything I do fit for him to see, and everything I say fit for him to hear.

All this I ask for your love's sake. Amen.

EVENING

O God, before I go to sleep, I want to thank you for
everything I have:

> For this bed in which I lie and this room with its
> comfort;
> For my home, for the food I eat, and the clothes
> I wear;
> For my books and my games and my hobbies and
> all my possessions;
> For my teachers and my father and my mother and
> my brothers and my sisters and my friends.

O God, I know that there is hardly one of these things
which I could get for myself. They are all given to me.

Help me to be grateful for them, and to try to deserve them
a little better.

This I ask for Jesus' sake. Amen.

Third Month: Second Week

MORNING

O God, you have given me life, and I know that you
want me to make something worthwhile out of it.
Help me

> To keep my body fit;
> To keep my mind keen;
> To keep my thoughts pure;
> To keep my words clean and true.

This I ask for Jesus' sake. Amen.

EVENING

Forgive me, O God, for all the wrong things which I have
done today.
Forgive me for

> Careless work;
> Inattentive study;
> Wasted time;
> Duties shirked.

O God, I really am sorry about all these things. Help
me to show that I am sorry by doing better tomorrow,
for Jesus' sake. Amen.

Third Month: Third Week

MORNING

O God, take control of me all through today.
Control my tongue
> so that I may speak
>> No angry word;
>> No cruel word;
>> No untrue word;
>> No ugly word.

Control my thoughts,
> so that I may think
>> No impure thoughts;
>> No bitter, envious, or jealous thoughts;
>> No selfish thoughts.

Control my actions,
> so that all through today
>> My work may be my best;
>> I may never be too busy to lend a hand to those who need it;
>> I may do nothing of which afterwards I would be ashamed.

All this I ask for Jesus' sake. Amen.

EVENING

O God, before I sleep, I ask you to bless the people I love.
Bless and protect
> My father and my mother;
> My brothers and my sisters;
> My friends and my teachers.

Bless and help
> Those who are sad and lonely;
> Those who are ill and who cannot sleep for pain;
> Those who are poor and forgotten and friendless;
> Those who are far away from home;
> Those who are in danger anywhere by land or sea
>   or in the air.

I know you love everyone and I ask you to bless everyone
  and to bless me, for Jesus' sake. Amen.

Third Month: Fourth Week

O God, all through today,
>   make me brave enough
>>   To show that I belong to you;
>>   To refuse any dishonest or dishonourable thing;
>>   To refuse to listen to any ugly or impure word;
>>   To do the right thing, even if others laugh at me.

Help me all through today really and truly to try to live
>   remembering Jesus all the time, and not caring what
>   anyone says so long as I am true to him.

This I ask for his sake. Amen.

O God, forgive me for all wrong things in today.

Forgive me for
>>   Disobedience to my parents;
>>   Failure to listen to my teachers;
>>   Disloyalty to my friends.

Forgive me for
>>   Being careless and inattentive in school;
>>   Being disobliging and selfish at home.

Forgive me for being
>>   A bad advertisement for my school and for my
>>   church;
>>   A bad example to others;
>>   A disappointment to you and to those who love me.

Help me to sleep well tonight and tomorrow give me
>   strength to do better.

This I ask for Jesus' sake. Amen.

Fourth Month: First Week

MORNING

Help me, O God, never to be envious, jealous, grumbling or discontented.

Help me never to take offence, if someone gets the prize which I thought I should have won, the place in the team which I thought should have been given to me, the honour which I thought I should have received.

Help me never to grudge anyone his or her success, and never to find pleasure in the sight of someone else's failure.

Help me to stop thinking of myself and of my own feelings as the most important things in the world, and help me always to think of others as much, and more than I think of myself.

Hear this my prayer for your love's sake. Amen.

EVENING

O God, help me to keep in purity my actions, my words, and my thoughts.

Help me to do nothing in secret which I would be ashamed to do openly, and keep me from doing things which I would have to hide and to conceal.

So do you control me that I may have every instinct and passion under complete control. Help me always to refuse to listen to anything which would soil my mind, and to reject every invitation to leave the way of honour.

Help me to speak nothing but the truth. Keep my words clean and let no foul or unclean or dirty word ever be in my mouth.

You have promised that the pure in heart will see you; grant me this purity, this privilege and this reward.

This I ask for Jesus' sake. Amen.

Fourth Month: Second Week

MORNING

Give me today, O God, the mind which can really learn.
Give me

> The attentive mind, that I may concentrate all
> the time on what I am hearing or doing;
>
> The retentive mind, that I may not hear and
> forget, but that I may grasp a thing and
> remember it;
>
> The open mind, that no prejudice may blind me
> to truth I do not wish to see;
>
> The eager mind, that I may not be content to re-
> main as I am, but that every day I may try to
> add something new to my store of knowledge
> and of skill, and something finer to my store
> of goodness.

This I ask for Jesus' sake. Amen.

EVENING

Forgive me, O God, for all the wrong things that have been
in my life today.
Forgive me

> For being careless and inattentive in learning;
>
> For being thoughtlessly or deliberately cruel and
> unkind to others;
>
> For hurting the people who love me most of all.
>
> For being disobedient to those whom I ought to
> obey, and for being disrespectful to those
> whom I ought to respect;
>
> For disobeying my conscience, and for doing the
> wrong thing when I knew the right thing.

Help me to show that I am really sorry by doing better
tomorrow and by not making the same mistakes again.
This I ask for Jesus' sake. Amen.

Fourth Month: Third Week

MORNING

O God, give me all the simple, basic things which will make me able to be a useful person in this world.

Help me to be

> Honest, so that people will be able absolutely to depend on my word;
>
> Conscientious, so that nothing that I do may ever be less than my best;
>
> Punctual, so that I may not waste the time of others by keeping them waiting for me.
>
> Reliable, so that I may never let people down when I promise to do something;
>
> With a sense of responsibility, so that I may always think of how my action will affect not only myself but others also.

Help me to live in the constant memory that you see and hear all that I do and say.

Hear this my prayer for your love's sake. Amen.

EVENING

O God, before I sleep I would remember others.
I ask you to bless
>The sick who will not sleep tonight;
>The sad who are very lonely tonight;
>Those in peril in the storms at sea;
>Those who are travelling by land or in the air;
>Those in prison and in disgrace;
>Those who have no house and no home of their own;
>Those on national service in the navy, the army, and the air force.

Bless all my friends and loved ones whose names I lay before you now ...
Hear this my prayer through Jesus Christ my Lord.
Amen.

Fourth Month: Fourth Week

MORNING

Help me, O God, to bear well the things which are hard to
bear.
Help me to bear

        Pain with cheerfulness and without complaint;

        Failure with the perseverance to go on trying
          until I succeed;

        Disappointment without bitterness and without
          resentment;

        Delays with the patience which has learned to
          wait;

        Criticism without losing my temper;

        Defeat without making excuses.
Help me to bear the yoke in my youth, that I may make
something worthwhile out of life when I grow up.
This I ask for Jesus' sake. Amen.

EVENING

Thank you, O God, for all the gifts which have made today and every day so wonderful.

Thank you for books to read, wise books to make me wise, books full of information to make me informed; great stories to thrill the heart and to linger in the memory; poetry with all its beauty.

Thank you for music of every kind, for dramas and for plays and for films, for pictures and for sculpture and for every lovely thing.

Thank you for games to play; for clubs and for fellowships where I can meet and talk and argue and play with others.

Thank you for

My school in which to learn;

My home in which to love and to be loved;

My church in which to worship.

Glory and thanks and praise be to you for all your kindness and your goodness to me.

Hear this my prayer for your love's sake. Amen.

Fifth Month: First Week

MORNING

Help me to be a good son/daughter, and to bring joy and
pride to my parents,

> To work hard, so that I will not disappoint those
> who have high hopes for me;
>
> To show that I am grateful for all that my parents
> have done for me, and sometimes to tell
> them so;
>
> To be obedient to them, and always to give them
> the loving respect I ought to give;
>
> Never to use my home simply for my own conve-
> nience, but to be a real partner in it, and to
> try to put into it more than I take out.

Help me always to honour my father and mother as your
law commands.

This I ask for Jesus' sake. Amen.

EVENING

Help me, O God, to be a good and a true friend,

> To be always loyal, and never to let my friends
> down;
>
> Never to talk about them behind their backs in a
> way in which I would not do before their faces;
>
> Never to betray a confidence or talk about the
> things about which I ought to be silent;
>
> Always to be ready to share everything I have;
>
> To be as true to my friends as I would wish them
> to be to me.

This I ask for the sake of him who is the greatest and the
truest of all friends, for Jesus' sake. Amen.

Fifth Month: Second Week

MORNING

Help me, O God, to be a good scholar and pupil of my
school,

> To study with concentration;
>
> To do my work with diligence and care;
>
> To be obedient and respectful to my teachers;
>
> To take my full part in the life and the activities
> of my school;
>
> To take full advantage of all the opportunities
> given to me to learn; and to make myself a
> good craftsman and a good citizen of my
> country when I leave school and go out to
> work;

This I ask for the sake of him who was the greatest of all
teachers, for Jesus' sake. Amen.

EVENING

Help me, O God, to be a good sportsman/woman and a
good member of my team,

> To accept discipline and to train strictly;
>
> To play hard but to play fair;
>
> To play the game for the good of the team and
> not for my own honour and glory.
>
> To obey instructions without arguing;
>
> Not to resent it if I am dropped from the team
> because someone else is preferred;
>
> To be a credit to my colours wherever I play and
> wherever I go.

This I ask for Jesus' sake. Amen.

Fifth Month: Third Week

MORNING

O Lord Jesus, help me to be a good follower of you,
>Always to follow your example;
>Always to ask what you want me to do before I decide to do anything;
>Always to ask for your help and your guidance;
>Always to remember that you are always with me to hear what I say, to see what I do, to keep me from doing wrong, and to give me the help I need to do the right:
>Never to be afraid to show my loyalty to you, and never to be ashamed to show that I belong to you;
>Never to forget all that you have done for me, and so to try to love you as you first loved me.

This I ask for your love's sake. Amen.

EVENING

O God, forgive me for all the things that I have left undone today; and forgive me for the things I have left half-finished and for the things which I never even started.

Forgive me for not saying 'Thank you' to the people who have helped me, and for not saying that I am sorry to the people whom I wronged and hurt.

Forgive me if I have hurt anyone, or disappointed anyone, or if I have caused anyone trouble, or if I have been a bad example to anyone.

Give me your help tomorrow, so that I may leave nothing undone of the things I ought to do, and so that I may do none of the things I ought not to do.

This I ask for your love's sake. Amen.

Fifth Month: Fourth Week

MORNING

Help me, O God, always to take the long view of things.
Keep me from ever doing on the impulse of the moment
things for which I would be very sorry afterwards.

Help me to remember that, even if at the moment I would
rather play and amuse myself than work or study, I
must accept the discipline of work, if I am to make
anything worthwhile out of life.

Especially keep me from any habits or indulgences or
pleasures which would injure others and hurt myself,
and which some day I would bitterly regret.

Help me to look beyond this moment, and even to look
beyond this world, and so help me to remember that
this life is not the end, and help me always to live in
such a way that, when this life does end, I may hear
you say, 'Well done!'

Hear this my prayer through Jesus Christ my Lord.
Amen.

EVENING

O God, tonight I want to pray to you for people who have
  to suffer and to sacrifice for their Christian faith.
I ask you to bless

> Missionaries who go out to other lands to tell the
> story of Jesus to those who have never heard
> it, and who have to endure discomforts, face
> dangers, and accept long months and years
> of separation from those whom they love;

> People who live in countries in which Christians
> are hated and hunted and persecuted for
> their faith, and specially Christians who live
> in countries in which they are persecuted
> and cruelly treated by others who also call
> themselves Christians but who belong to a
> different Church;

> People who live or work in circumstances in
> which they are laughed at and even despised
> for trying to live a Christian life.

This I ask for your love's sake. Amen.

Sixth Month: First Week

'The fruit of the Spirit is love, joy, peace, patience, kindness, goodness, faithfulness, gentleness and self-control.' That is what Paul wrote to his friends in the Churches of Galatia (Galatians 5:22, 23). Let us all through this month ask God to give us these lovely things in our lives.

O God, give me in my life the fruit of love.

Help me to love you so much that I will never forget all that you have given me and all that you have done for me. Help me always to remember that you gave me life and everything that makes life worth living, and that you gave me Jesus to be my Friend, my Example, my Master, and my Saviour. Help me to love my fellow-men so much that I will no longer be selfish and self-centred, but that I will find the way to happiness in doing things for others. This I ask for your love's sake. Amen.

O God, give me in my life the fruit of joy.

Help me always to be happy and cheerful. Help me still to smile even when things go wrong. Help me always to look on the bright side of things, and always to remember that, even when things are at their worst, there is still something to be thankful for. Don't let me grumble and complain; don't let me be a pessimist and a wet blanket.

And help me to find my happiness, not in doing what I want, but in doing what you want, and not in thinking of myself, but in thinking of others, through Jesus Christ my Lord. Amen.

Sixth Month: Second Week

O God, give me in my life the fruit of peace.

Help me to take things calmly. Help me not to get into a panic when things go wrong. Help me not to worry but to take things as they come, a day at a time. Help me not to be nervous but to keep cool, when I have something difficult or important to do. Help me never to lose my temper, no matter how annoying things or people may be.

Keep me calm and steady, so that I will never collapse, and so that others may be able to rely on me when they are up against it. This I ask for Jesus' sake. Amen.

O God, give me in my life the fruit of patience.

Help me to have patience at my work and study, so that I will never give in but always persevere.

Help me to have patience with people, so that I may never lose my temper and never grow cross or irritable, or blaze into angry words. Help me to have patience when things are slow to come and slow to happen.

Help me to have patience not to give up, when something takes a long time to do, and when it does not come out right the first or the second time.

Help me to remember that everything worth doing is hard to do; that everything worth getting is hard to get; that everything worth being is hard to be, but that the struggle and the effort are worthwhile in the end.

This I ask for Jesus' sake. Amen.

Sixth Month: Third Week

O God, give me in my life the fruit of kindness.

Make me quick to see what I can do for others, and make me eager and willing to do it. Make me always obliging and always willing to lend a hand. Help me never to be mean, but always to be ready to share everything I have, even if I have not got very much.

Help me never to speak unkind words and never to do cruel deeds. Help me to think the best of others, and always to be more willing to forgive than to condemn.

Help me to be as kind to others as I would wish them to be to me.

Hear this my prayer for your love's sake. Amen.

O God, give me in my life the fruit of goodness.

Help me to be in everything I do and say a good example to others, and help me never to do anything which would make it easier for someone else to go wrong.

Keep my words honest and pure. Keep my actions fit for you to see, and help me never to do anything that I would wish to keep secret, and that I would be afraid that other people would find out about. Keep all my thoughts clean, so that even the most secret of them would bear the full light of day.

And in everything keep me from pride and from self-conceit; and help me to think, not of what I know, but of what I don't know, not of what I have done, but of what I have still to do; not of what I am, but of what I ought to be.

Hear this my prayer for Jesus' sake. Amen.

Sixth Month: Fourth Week

O God, give me in my life the fruit of faithfulness.

Keep me always true to myself, true to my friends, true to those who love me and true to you.

Grant that nothing may ever make me tell a lie. If I give my promise, grant that nothing may ever make me break it. If I say that I will do something, grant that others may be able to rely absolutely on me to do it. Help me always to stand by my friends and never to let them down, and help me never to grieve or to disappoint those who love me and those whom I love.

Make me so straight, so honourable and so true that everyone will be able to trust me in small things and in great alike. This I ask through Jesus Christ my Lord. Amen.

O God, give me in my life the fruit of gentleness.

Help me never to speak an angry or a cruel word, and never to do a hurting or a wounding deed.

Grant that I may never find any pleasure in anything which would hurt any person or any animal.

Help me to be as careful of the feelings of others as I would wish them to be of mine.

Help me not to be too rough and boisterous in my behaviour with those who are not so strong as I am. And make me specially gentle and thoughtful to those who are sick and sad and old and weak and easily hurt.

This I ask for your love's sake. Amen.

O God, give me in my life the fruit of self-control.

Please take control of me so that I will be able to control myself.

Help me always to control my temper and my tongue. Help me always to control my feelings and my impulses.

Grant that I may never be swept away in some moment of passion into doing something which would hurt anyone else and which all my life I would regret.

Help me to control even my thoughts, so that no bitter thought, no unforgiving thought, no jealous thought, no ugly or unclean thought may ever get into my mind.

Make me master of myself for I know that, unless I can master myself I can never make anything worthwhile out of life.

Hear this my prayer for your love's sake. Amen.

Seventh Month: First Week

MORNING

Lord Jesus, help me to remember that you are always
with me.

Help me to do nothing which would grieve you to see,
and nothing which I would be ashamed to think that
you should see me doing.

When I am tempted, help me always to ask you for
strength to do the right thing and to resist the wrong
thing.

When I don't know what to do, help me to turn to you
and ask you for your advice.

When I am frightened and lonely, help me to feel that
you are there, and to know that with you I don't ever
need to be afraid.

Help me to go through life with you as my Friend and
my Companion all the time.

This I ask for your love's sake. Amen.

EVENING

O God, forgive me for all the things in me which have
kept today from being what it might have been.
Forgive me for being
> Inattentive at school;
> Disobliging at home;
> Bad-tempered with my friends;
> Selfish and thoughtless in my conduct.
Help me tomorrow
> To concentrate on learning;
> To honour my father and my mother;
> To be generous and unselfish in everything;
> To be a good comrade to all my friends.
So help me to please you, and not to disappoint those who
love me.
This I ask for Jesus' sake. Amen.

Seventh Month: Second Week

MORNING

Help me today, O God,

> To keep my temper and to control my tongue;
>
> To keep my thoughts from wandering and my mind from straying;
>
> To quarrel with no one and to be friends with everyone.

So bring me to the end of today with nothing to be sorry for, and with nothing left undone; through Jesus Christ my Lord. Amen.

EVENING

O God, thank you for taking care of me all through today.

Thank you for making me able to go out in the morning in good health, and thank you for giving me my home and my father and mother to come back to.

Thank you

> For all that I have learned today;
>
> For all the games that I have played today;
>
> For all the friends that I have met today.

And thank you for Jesus my Master and my Friend.

Help me to sleep soundly tonight, and to waken fit for work and play tomorrow; through Jesus Christ my Lord. Amen.

Seventh Month: Third Week

MORNING

Whatever happens today, help me to keep cheerful.
Help me

> Not to grumble when things go wrong;
> Not to be discouraged when things are difficult;
> Not to get annoyed when I don't get my own way;
> Not to sulk if I get a row for anything wrong that I have done.

Help me, hail, rain, or shine, to keep smiling, so that I may be what you want me to be – a light of the world.
This I ask for your love's sake. Amen.

EVENING

O God, I don't want to pray for myself tonight; I want to pray for others.
I ask you to bless

> Those who are ill, and whose pain is worse at night;
> Those who are sad, and who are specially lonely at night;
> Those who are in strange towns and countries, and who are missing their own homes and their own people;
> Those in danger at sea, or in the air, or on the land;
> Doctors and nurses, awake and helping others, while we sleep;
> All the people I love, and all the people who love me.

And bless me and keep me safe all through the night until the morning comes again; through Jesus Christ my Lord. Amen.

Seventh Month: Fourth Week

MORNING

O God, help me never to allow any habit to get such a grip
of me that I cannot break it.

Specially keep me from all habits which would injure my
body or my mind.

Help me always to do my best with your help to keep my
body fit and healthy, and my mind clean and pure.

Help me at present to discipline and to train myself, to
learn and to study, so that some day I may be able to
do something worthwhile for the world and for you;
through Jesus Christ my Lord. Amen.

EVENING

O God, forgive me for all the wrong things that I have done today.

Forgive me

> For blaming others for things which were entirely my own fault;
>
> For being rude, and discourteous, and bad-tempered, especially at home;
>
> For being rough, and unkind, and unjust.

Forgive me

> For the things which I should have done and have not done;
>
> For the times I lost my temper and my patience;
>
> For the lessons I have left unprepared and the tasks I have left half-done or badly done;
>
> For the things I promised to do and did not do.

The trouble is that I know what I ought to do, and I really mean to do it, but somehow it does not turn out that way.

Forgive me, and help me tomorrow

> To do what I know I ought to do,
>
> And to be what I know I ought to be.

This I ask for your love's sake. Amen.

Eighth Month: First Week

MORNING

Even before Christianity came into the world men have
always believed that the four greatest virtues are
WISDOM, COURAGE, JUSTICE and SELF-CONTROL.
Let us ask God to help us to have them in our lives.

O God, help me to have in my life the virtues which all
men value and admire.

Give me wisdom always to know
What I ought to do;
What I ought to say;
Where I ought to go.

Give me courage,
To do the right thing when it is difficult;
If need be, to be laughed at for my faith;
Never to be ashamed to show my loyalty to you.

Give me justice,
Always to be fair in thought and word and action;
Always to think of the rights of others as much as
of my own;
Never to be content when anyone is being unjustly
treated.

Give me self-control,
Always to have my impulses, passions and emo-
tions under perfect control;
Never to be swept into doing things for which I
would be sorry;
Never to do anything which would hurt others,
grieve those who love me, or bring shame to
myself.

Hear this my prayer for your love's sake. Amen.

EVENING

Forgive me, O God,

      For the time I have wasted today;

      For the people I have hurt today;

      For the tasks I have shirked today.

Help me

      Not to be discouraged when things are difficult;

      Not to be content with second bests;

      To do better tomorrow than I have done today.

And help me always to remember that Jesus is with me

    and that I am not trying all alone.

This I ask for Jesus' sake. Amen.

Eighth Month: Second Week

MORNING

O God, keep me from allowing any habit to get such a
grip of me that I can't stop it.

Keep me from becoming so fond of any pleasure that I
can't do without it.

Keep me from allowing myself to become lazy, and from
getting into a state in which I don't really care whether
things are well or badly done.

Keep me from allowing myself to do things which would
make it easier for me to go wrong and which would be
a bad example to others.

Help me to live in purity and in self-discipline, and in the
memory that you are always with me to see what I
do, and to help me to overcome wrong and to do the
right; through Jesus Christ my Lord. Amen.

EVENING

Forgive me, O God, for all the opportunities that I have
missed today: opportunities to learn more; to gain a
little more knowledge or skill for my mind; to help
people who need help; to say a word of praise or
thanks or congratulation; to show those who love me
that I love them.

Help me to remember that opportunities so often only
come once, and help me from this time on to seize
them when they come; through Jesus Christ my Lord.
Amen.

Eighth Month: Third Week

O God, your word tells me that, whatever my hand
finds to do, I must do it with my might.
Help me today to concentrate with my whole attention
on whatever I am doing, and keep my thoughts from
wandering and my mind from straying.
> When I am studying,
>> help me to study with my whole mind.
> When I am playing,
>> help me to play with my whole heart.

Help me to do one thing at a time, and to do it well.
This I ask for Jesus' sake. Amen.

Thank you, O God, for everything that has happened
today:
> For the good things which have made me happy;
> For the not-so-good things which have taught me
>> that I can't always be getting my own way;
> For successes to give me happy things to remember;
> For failures to keep me humble;
> For time at work, at school, at games,
>> with my friends and in my own home.

And thank you for this minute with you. Help me to go
to sleep thinking about you that I may rise tomorrow
to live obedient and true to you; through Jesus Christ
my Lord. Amen.

Eighth Month: Fourth Week

MORNING

O God, help me to be cheerful all through today,
>Whatever I have to do, help me to do it with a smile.

O God, help me to be diligent all through today,
>Whatever I have to do, help me to do my best.

O God, help me to be kind all through today,
>Whatever I have to do, help me not to be too busy
to help someone else.

O God, help me to be brave all through today,
>Whatever I have to do, help me to face it and not
to dodge it.

O God, help me to be reverent all through today,
>Whatever I have to do, help me to remember that
you see me, and help me to make every word
fit for you to hear, and every bit of work fit to
offer to you.

This I ask for your love's sake. Amen.

EVENING

O God, bless all the people who are in trouble tonight,
those who cannot sleep because they are ill and
in pain, or because they are old and lonely, or
because they are worried and nervous and anxious.

Bless any who are in danger.

Bless those who must work at night,
>doctors on call, nurses in hospital and infirmary
wards, policemen on the beat, those called out to
accidents, fires, shipwrecks.

Bless me now, and help me to sleep well tonight and to
waken tomorrow to live strong and true; through
Jesus Christ my Lord. Amen.

Ninth Month: First Week

MORNING

O God, my Father, thank you for all the ordinary, everyday things of life.

Thank you,

> For food and for a good appetite to enjoy it;
> For games and for physical fitness to play them;
> For lessons and for a mind to learn and to think,
> and for a memory to remember;
> For work and for strength and skill to do it.

Help me always

> To keep my body clean and fit;
> To keep my mind keen and alert;
> To give my heart to you, because you have loved
> me so much and have done so much for me.

This I ask for Jesus' sake. Amen.

EVENING

O God, before I go to sleep tonight I am looking back
across today.

Thank you,

> For any new thing I have learned today;
> For any good thing I have been able to do today;
> For any happiness I have brought today to those
> who love me and who want me to do well.

Forgive me

> For anything I have shirked today;
> For anything I have put off today;
> For anything which I could have done better
> today;
> For anyone whom I have hurt or disappointed
> today.

Help me to sleep well tonight and to do better tomorrow.
This I ask for your love's sake. Amen.

Ninth Month: Second Week

O God, my Father, give me all through today sound sense to see what it is right to do, and strength of will and purpose to do it. And, if I am not able to do it the first time, give me perseverance to keep on trying.

O God, my Father, give me all through today an eye which is quick to see what I can do for others, and willingness to do it.

Help me not to do things with a grudge; and help me to do what I am told to do at once, and not to need to be told to do it again and again.

Help me today to bring happiness wherever I go, so that I may find my own happiness in making others happy; through Jesus Christ my Lord. Amen.

O God, thank you for all the people who have been kind to me today.

Thank you for the people who have patience with me when I am irritating and annoying, and who don't lose their temper with me when I lose mine with them.

Thank you for the people who have patience with me when I am slow to learn and slow to take things in, and who don't give me up as hopeless, when I seem to make no progress at all.

Thank you for those who give me, not what I deserve, but far more than I deserve.

Thank you for those who keep on loving me even when I hurt and disappoint them.

Help me to try to bring joy to those who do so much for me, by trying to be what they want me to be; through Jesus Christ my Lord. Amen.

Ninth Month: Third Week

O God, help me to think all through today in every word
and in every action and in every situation of what
Jesus would do.

Help me to think of how Jesus went to school and learned
and grew in wisdom, just as I must do.

Help me to think how he worked in the carpenter's shop
and learned a trade, just as I must do.

Help me to remember how he obeyed his parents, just
as I must do.

Help me to remember how he found people unjust and
unfair and unsympathetic and unkind, just as may
happen to me.

Help me to remember how his friends let him down,
just as may happen to me.

Help me to remember that he loved us all so much that
he gave for us everything he had, even his life, just
as I ought to do.

He has left us an example that we should follow in his
steps. Help me to follow in his steps all through today.

This I ask for your love's sake. Amen.

EVENING

O God, forgive me for all the things which have defeated
me today.
For the times

> When I knew that I ought to do something, and
> when I was too lazy to do it;
>
> When I knew that I ought to help someone, and
> when I was too lazy to be bothered;
>
> When I knew that I ought to keep quiet, and
> when I let my tongue run away with me;
>
> When I knew that I ought to keep my temper, and
> when I let it flare up and blaze out;
>
> When I knew I ought to speak, and when I
> remained silent because I was too much of a
> coward to speak.

O God, I always start in the morning meaning to do so
well, and I seem always to finish at night after doing
so badly. Forgive me; help me; and, whatever happens, don't let me stop trying.
This I ask for Jesus' sake. Amen.

Ninth Month: Fourth Week

FOR SUNDAY MORNING

O God, help me to remember that this is your day, and
help me to use it differently from the other days.

Help me to use it to learn something more about Jesus and
to come to know him a little better.

Help me to use it to go to church to sing and pray and
listen and worship with those who are the friends of
Jesus.

Help me to use it to do something for others – those who
are ill, those who are old, and those who are lonely.

Help me to use Sunday in such a way as to help me to
live better through all the other days of the week:
through Jesus Christ my Lord. Amen.

BEFORE GOING TO CHURCH

O God, in church today help me to listen, to understand
and to remember.

Help me to go to church reverently, because the church
is your house and you are specially there.

When we all pray, grant that it may be just like speaking to you.

When I listen, help me to concentrate so that I will really
hear and take in and remember what is said.

And then help me to go out and to put into practice all
you tell me in your house.

This I ask for your love's sake. Amen.

Tenth Month: First Week

MORNING

O God, my Father, help me today not to let anyone or anything stop me from being what I ought to be and doing what I ought to do.

> Even if people are nasty to me, help me to be courteous to them.
>
> Even if people are unkind to me, help me to be loving and kind to them.
>
> Even if people hurt me or insult me or injure me, help me to forgive them as Jesus forgave those who were crucifying him.
>
> Even if things and people make it very difficult for me to do what I know I ought to do, help me still at least to try to do it.

Lord Jesus, help me to live today in perfect loyalty and obedience to you.

This I ask for your love's sake. Amen.

EVENING

Forgive me, O God, for everything in which I have failed today.

Forgive me for

Losing my temper when I should have controlled it;

Allowing my tongue to run away with me when I should have kept quiet;

Allowing myself to have bitter feelings about someone else;

Refusing to listen to good advice and for resenting correction when I deserved it.

Forgive me for

Failing to do things as well as I could have done them,

Failing to finish the tasks I should have finished;

Failing to work my hardest at my lessons and my work, and to play my hardest at my games.

Forgive me for everything that I meant to do and failed to do, and for everything that I meant not to do and did.

This I ask for Jesus' sake. Amen.

Tenth Month: Second Week

O God, help me to live well today.
Help me
> To do my work diligently;
> To face my temptations victoriously;
> To play my games whole-heartedly;
> To bear my disappointments cheerfully;
> To face my difficulties manfully;
> To give all the help I can to all the people I can
> willingly;
> To obey you faithfully;
> And to follow Jesus loyally.

All this I ask for Jesus' sake. Amen.

EVENING

O God, thank you for giving me another day of life.
Thank you for
> The things I have learned today;
> The games I have played today;
> The friends I have met today;

Thank you for
> The love and care I have received today in my home;
> The teaching and training I have received today in my school;
> The loyalty and friendship I have received today from my comrades.

Thank you most of all for Jesus,
> The Example whom I must copy;
> The Friend who never leaves me;
> The Saviour who forgives me and makes me able to live well.

Hear this my prayer, and give me always a grateful heart; through Jesus Christ my Lord. Amen.

Tenth Month: Third Week

O God, I ask you to bless all the people who today will have to do very difficult things and face very great responsibilities:

> Statesmen and women who will have to make decisions on which the welfare of nations and even of the world depends;
>
> Doctors and surgeons in whose hands and whose skill are the lives of men and women and boys and girls;
>
> Those whose job makes them responsible for the safety and the lives of others;
>
> Those who are in positions in which by speaking or by writing or by their example they can influence the lives of thousands of people;
>
> Bless all such.

Bless me. You have given me this life and I am responsible to you for how I use it. Help me to use every moment of today's time and every ounce of today's strength wisely and well; through Jesus Christ my Lord. Amen.

EVENING

O God, help me to sleep well tonight.

And bless those for whom there will be no sleep tonight:

> Policemen on the beat;
>
> Workers on the night-shift;
>
> Sailors at sea, train drivers on the railways, drivers on the roads, pilots in the air;
>
> All who through the night look after the essential public services on which our convenience and comfort depend;
>
> Doctors and surgeons and nurses, easing the pain or fighting for the life of those who are desperately ill;
>
> Parents with children who cannot sleep.

O God, I know that you never slumber or sleep. Through the dark hours give me sleep and watch over me while I sleep, and be with those who work while others sleep.

This I ask for Jesus' sake. Amen.

Tenth Month: Fourth Week

MORNING

O God, give me all through today

> Grace willingly to say Yes, when I am asked to help someone else;
>
> Strength resolutely to say No, when I am tempted or persuaded to do anything that is wrong;
>
> Patience to say to myself Wait, when I am in too big a hurry;
>
> Resolution to say Now, when I am inclined to put off till some future time what should be done today;
>
> Obedience to say to you, Lord, What do you want me to do? in every choice which comes to me today.

Hear this my prayer through Jesus Christ my Lord. Amen.

EVENING

O God, thank you for today.

Thank you for

> Lessons and tasks which stretched my mind, and made it able to cope with still more difficult things;
>
> Training and games which left me tired, but fit for bigger efforts;
>
> Kindness which touched my heart and made me love people and be grateful to them more than ever;
>
> Anything in the world or in the things which happened today which made me think of you.

Thank you for the good things which I will never forget, and forgive me for the bad things which I would like to forget; through Jesus Christ my Lord. Amen.

Eleventh Month: First Week

MORNING

O God, my Father, help me to do the things which are very
    difficult for anyone to do.
        To be obedient,
            When I would like my own way;
        To persevere,
            When I am tired and discouraged,
            And when I would like to give up;
        To study,
            When I would like to be out playing games;
        To help with the work of the house,
            When I think that it is a nuisance,
            And when I can't be bothered;
        To keep my temper,
            When I would like to blaze out,
            And tell people just what I think of them;
        To forgive,
            When I am feeling hurt and sore and bitter;
            Help me to do these things.
At all times help me to find my happiness in obeying
    you.
This I ask for your love's sake. Amen.

EVENING

Forgive me, O God, for all the wrong things I have done today.

Forgive me

For forgetting the things I ought to have remembered;

For failing to do the things I promised to do;

For being inattentive to the things to which I should have listened;

For being careless with the work on which I should have concentrated;

Forgive me, O God.

Forgive me

For doing things which I knew would annoy people;

For behaving in a way that I knew would hurt people;

For doing things that I knew would disappoint people;

Forgive me, O God.

O God, when I look back, I can see now how foolish and how wrong I have been. Forgive me, and help me not to do the same things again.

This I ask for Jesus' sake. Amen.

Eleventh Month: Second Week

Help me, O God, not to waste my time and energy on useless things.

Help me

> Not to envy others their gifts,
>> But to make the best of the gifts I have;
>
> Never to wish that I was someone else or some-
> where else,
>> But to do the best I can as I am, and where I am;
>
> Never to be jealous of anyone else,
>> But to be glad when others do well,
>
> Not to worry about things,
>> But to take them as they come;
>
> Never to be lost in dreams and schemes and plans,
>> Without doing anything to make them come
>> true.

Help me to use my strength and my time wisely, bravely
and unselfishly, so that I will make the best of life for
myself and for others; through Jesus Christ my Lord.
Amen.

EVENING

O God, forgive me
> For hurting my parents today;
> For causing trouble to my teachers today;
> For failing to help my friends today.

Forgive me
> For being discourteous in my conduct today;
> For being unkind in my words today;
> For being unjust in my thoughts today.

Forgive me
> For the things I put off;
> For the things I did in too big a hurry to do them
>   well;
> For the things I have left half-done;
> For the things I should not have done at all.

Forgive me, and help me to do better tomorrow: for Jesus' sake. Amen.

Eleventh Month: Third Week

MORNING

O God, my Father, thank you for the world in which
I live.
Thank you
For all the beautiful things in it;
For all the interesting things in it;
For all the useful things in it.
Thank you for the life which you have given me.
Thank you for
My body to act;
My mind to think;
My memory to remember;
My heart to love.
Thank you for giving me
So many things to enjoy;
So many things to learn;
So many things to do;
So many people to love.
Help me never to do anything which would make the
world uglier or people sadder. Help me always to
add something to the world's beauty and to the world's
joy: through Jesus Christ my Lord. Amen.

EVENING

O God, bless all the people who are in trouble tonight.
Bless

> Those who are sad because someone they loved
> has died today;
>
> Those who are anxious because someone they
> love is ill today;
>
> Those who are lonely because someone they love
> left home today.

Bless

> Those who are tired because they have too much
> to do;
>
> Those who are poor and badly paid, and who have
> to do without the things they really need;
>
> Those who are unhappy because someone has
> been unkind and cruel to them.

Help me never to be selfish and never to forget all about
the people who are not so fortunate as I am. Help me
always to remember the needs of others and to do what
I can to help; through Jesus Christ my Lord. Amen.

Eleventh Month: Fourth Week

MORNING

Give me, O God, a sense of responsibility.
Give me

> A sense of responsibility to myself,
>> So that I may never waste the gifts which you
>> have given to me;
>
> A sense of responsibility to my parents,
>> So that I may do something to try to repay
>> them for all the love and the care they have
>> given to me;
>
> A sense of responsibility to my teachers,
>> So that all their patient teaching of me may
>> not go for nothing;
>
> A sense of responsibility to my friends,
>> So that I may never disappoint them;
>
> A sense of responsibility to those who have gone
> before me,
>> So that I may never forget what my freedom
>> and liberty cost, and so that I may hand on
>> still finer the heritage and the tradition into
>> which I have entered;
>
> A sense of responsibility to the world,
>> So that I may put into life more than I take
>> out;
>
> A sense of responsibility to Jesus,
>> So that I may always remember that he
>> loved me and gave himself for me.

Help me to remember what I have received, and to use
what I have, and so to make what I ought out of this
life of mine, which cost so much.
This I ask for Jesus' sake. Amen.

EVENING

Forgive me, O God, for all the times when I was a trouble and a nuisance to people today.

Forgive me

> For times when I was stubborn and obstinate;
>
> For times when I was careless and forgetful;
>
> For times when I was disobliging and unhelpful;
>
> For times when I was far slower to learn than I need have been;
>
> For times when I was late and kept people waiting;
>
> For times when I argued when I should have kept quiet;
>
> For times when I got in the way, and hindered people and kept them back;
>
> For times when I made things unpleasant when I did not get my own way.

Help me from now on always to make things easier and not more difficult for the people with whom I live and work, and to help people on the way instead of getting in their way.

This I ask for your love's sake. Amen.

Twelfth Month: First Week

MORNING

O God, give me a sense of responsibility.
Keep me

From doing things without thinking;

From leaving an untidy mess behind me wherever
I go;

From being carelessly or deliberately destructive;

From not caring how much worry and anxiety I
cause other people;

From not even beginning to realize all that I get,
and all that is done for me, and all that it costs
to give it to me;

From failing to grasp the opportunities which are
offered to me;

From failing to realize the difference between the
things which are important and the things
which do not matter.

Help me

Always to use my time and my life wisely and well;

Always to be considerate of others;

Always to realize all that is done for me, and to
show by my good and cheerful conduct that I
am grateful for it.

Hear this my prayer for Jesus' sake. Amen.

EVENING

O God, I know that you like a good workman, and I
don't think that I have been very good today.
I am remembering now
       Things I haven't done at all;
       Things I have left half-done and unfinished;
       Things I didn't do very well, not nearly as well as
          I could have done them;
       Things I did with a grudge;
       Things I put off, and things I refused to do.
Forgive me for all bad workmanship, and help me to
do better tomorrow; through Jesus Christ my Lord.
Amen.

Twelfth Month: Second Week

MORNING

Help me, O God, not to be impatient when older people
tell me what to do and what not to do, even though
they often tell me to do things I don't want to do,
and to stop doing things I do want to do.

Help me to remember that they know what life is like,
and that they know from experience the things which
are wise and the things which are bound to cause
trouble.

And help me to remember, when I think that they are
hard on me, that it is not because they don't like me
but because they do like me, and because they want
to save me from mistakes and to see me do well.

So help me always to be obedient and always to listen
to advice.

This I ask for Jesus' sake. Amen.

EVENING

Forgive me, O God, for everything that has gone wrong
today.

Forgive me

>   For being cheeky to my parents;
>   For being careless with my lessons;
>   For quarrelling with my friends;
>   For causing people extra work and extra trouble;
>   For grumbling and complaining about things
>   which I knew that I would have to do in the
>   end anyway.

Help me tomorrow to make life more pleasant for myself
and for everyone I live with and everyone I meet;
through Jesus Christ my Lord. Amen.

Twelfth Month: Third Week

MORNING

Give me, O God, a will that is strong and steady.
Help me

> Not to give up so easily,
>> but to stick at things until I succeed in doing
>> them;
>
> Not to be so easily annoyed,
>> but to keep calm, and to take things as they
>> come;
>
> Not to be so easily led,
>> but to be able to stand alone, and, if necessary,
>> to say No, and to keep on saying No;
>
> Not to lose interest so quickly,
>> but to concentrate on everything I do,
>> and to finish everything I begin.

Give me a will strong enough always to choose the right,
and never to be persuaded to anything that is wrong;
through Jesus Christ my Lord. Amen.

EVENING

Bless those who are ill, and who cannot sleep tonight
because of their pain.

Bless those who are in hospitals, in infirmaries, and in
nursing homes; and bless the doctors and the nurses
who are trying to help and to cure them.

Bless those who are sad and lonely.

Bless those who are in prison and all those who are in
any kind of trouble or disgrace.

Bless those who are far away from home, amongst strange
people in a strange place.

Bless all those whom I love and all those who love me.

Bless me and help me to sleep well tonight.

This I ask for Jesus' sake. Amen.

Twelfth Month: Fourth Week

O God, bless my school, the headteacher, the teachers, the pupils and everybody in it.

Help us all to work so hard and to play so well that everyone will respect and admire our school.

When I am in school, help me to be a good and attentive pupil, and, when I am out of school, help me always to behave in such a way that I will always be a credit to the badge and to the colours which I wear.

Help me to remember all the time that I am at school that I am preparing myself to be a good citizen of this country, and a good servant of yours; and to that end help me

> To discipline my mind to be wise;
> To train my body to be fit;
> To equip my life to be useful.

Hear this my prayer for your love's sake. Amen.

EVENING

O God, thank you for keeping me safe all day today from the time I got up in the morning until now it is time to go to bed and to sleep.

Thank you,

For giving me health and strength to work and to play;

For giving me food to eat, clothes to wear, and a home to live in;

For giving me parents to care for me, teachers to instruct me, friends to work and to play with me;

For bringing me to this night, and for giving me sleep and a bed to sleep in;

For giving me Jesus to be my Master and my Friend, and to be with me all through the day and all through the night.

And grant that the memory of his presence may keep me from all wrong things by day and from all fear by night.

This I ask for your love's sake. Amen.

More Prayers for
Young People

Preface

I should be sadly lacking in courtesy if I did not express my thanks to those who have helped in the writing of this book.

First of all, I wish to thank Lady Collins who in the first instance suggested the book and then waited with patience for it. Secondly, I wish to thank my secretary, Mrs D. Hamilton, who typed it and whose advice was always helpful.

As to the book itself, each day's contents begin with a prayer written for the occasion, and then a scripture reading, and finally there is a prayer written by someone famous in history or in literature. The Bible readings over the six weeks are designed to form a life of Christ.

It is my hope and prayer that this book may be of some use to young people. It is only designed to be a beginning and the aim of the book will be realized if the time comes when those who use it can throw it away and make their own prayers to God.

William Barclay
Glasgow, June 1976

Introduction

On Praying

The great men and women said their prayers themselves and encouraged others to do so. Charles Dickens wrote the following letter to his youngest son who went out to Australia in 1868:

> I need not tell you that I love you dearly and am very, very sorry in my heart to part with you. I have put a New Testament among your books because it is the best book that ever was, or will be, known in the world. As your brothers have gone away one by one I have written to each such words as I am now writing to you, entreating them all to guide themselves by this book. Only one thing more, never abandon the practice of private prayer. I know the comfort of it.

So Dickens writes to his son never to abandon the practice of private prayer. Aldous Huxley was one of the greatest of the moderns and in the second volume of his biography by Sybille Bedford, it is said of him that he was asked once, 'Aldous, do you pray?' He answered: 'I always say my prayers – in the simplest possible words, I always begin "Now I lay me down to sleep" – and my prayers are nearly always answered.' So then, the great men and women in every generation have said their prayers, and this is what this book is designed to help you to do.

The first question we ask about our prayers is 'What shall I say?' This book is designed to tell you what to say, but it is also meant to make you able to speak for yourself, and its aim will be realized if the day comes when you throw it away and need it no longer. In prayer we can say anything we like to God because we can talk to him in the simplest and most straightforward manner.

Another question that we must ask is 'How will I keep my thoughts from wandering?' It is very difficult to think of any subject for any length of time. In fact, it has been said that it is impossible to think of the one thing, and nothing but the one thing, for even as short a time as two minutes. When we pray we find this, that and the next thought coming into our minds. Frank Boreham tells how C. Aubrey Price gave him a bit of good advice, and this was 'Always pray *aloud*'. It is much easier to concentrate when we are actually speaking aloud than when we are merely speaking into ourselves.

It will help to concentrate our thoughts if we pray in an orderly way. There are five different kinds of prayer:

the prayer of approach;
the prayer of confession;
the prayer of thanksgiving;
the prayer of petition;
the prayer of intercession.

In the prayer of approach we make ourselves aware of the presence of God around us and about us. In the prayer of confession we ask God's forgiveness for the wrong things that we have done. In the prayer of thanksgiving we give thanks for the many gifts with which we are surrounded. In the prayer of petition we bring our own special needs and desires to God. In the prayer of intercession we pray for other people.

The next question we ask is 'What can I expect when I pray?' When we pray we ought to be quite sure what we are doing. Very often we pray to God to save us from something or to take something away from us. The real prayer is not so much to ask God to be saved from things. The real prayer is for help to conquer whatever situation we are in – not to be liberated from the thing, but to overcome it.

The next question we might ask is 'When do I pray?' Ideally, the best time to pray is night and morning, but it is possible to pray anywhere. Sir Thomas Browne, the famous physician, says:

> *I have resolved to pray more and to pray always, to pray in all places where quietness inviteth, in the house, on the highway, in the streets; and to know no street or passage in this city that may not witness that I have not forgotten God.*

Sir Thomas Browne meant that even going about his daily business he could pray anywhere, and so can we.

The next question we may well ask is 'What must be my physical attitude in prayer?' We must not think there is any one answer to this question. The only answer which is valid for everyone is that we ought to pray in a position in which our body is comfortable, because if we do not some slight discomfort will interfere with our concentration, and we will think more of the discomfort than of the prayer.

Another mistake that we make regularly is that we think too much of prayer in the sense of us talking to God. In prayer there should be just as much of listening to God. Prayer is not a monologue, it is a dialogue. Brother Lawrence said that his aim was 'that we should establish ourselves in a sense of God's presence by continual conversing with him', and conversation with anyone demands silence as well as speaking. We have therefore in prayer not only to talk to God but to listen to God.

It will be of the greatest possible help to prayer if we succeed in living a life in which we are always conscious of God; not just conscious of him in the crisis or the emergency, but conscious of him always. Someone has put it this way. 'The commandment says "Remember the Sabbath Day, to keep it holy", but we ought to say "Remember the week day, to keep it holy".' Every day is a day when we ought to pray, and every place is a place where we ought to pray, and it comes most easily when, wherever we are, we are aware of the presence of God.

I hope you will find this book useful, but I would also hope, as I have already said, that you will soon arrive at a stage when you don't need it, when you can make your own prayers and when you can put this book away, having finished with its usefulness.

Daily Prayers

Monday: First Week

Help me, O God, to go out to begin this week's work in your
    company.
Help me to remember that you are always with me, and so
    help me to make everything I do and everything I say
    fit for you to see and to hear.
Help me never to do or to say anything which would bring
    sorrow to those who live with me, grief to you, or shame
    to myself; through Jesus Christ my Lord. Amen.

THE BIRTH OF JESUS

This was the way in which the birth of Jesus took place.
Mary his mother was pledged to be married to Joseph, but,
before they became man and wife, it was discovered that
she was going to have a child, as a result of the action of
the Holy Spirit. Although Joseph, her intended husband,
was a man who strictly kept the Law, he had no desire
publicly to humiliate her, so he wished to divorce her
secretly. While he was planning to do this, an angel of the
Lord appeared to him in a dream. 'Joseph, son of David,'
the angel said, 'do not hesitate to marry Mary, for it is as
a result of the action of the Holy Spirit that she is going to
have a child. She will have a son, and you must call him
by the name Jesus, for it is he who will save his people from
their sins.' All this happened that the statement made by
the Lord through the prophet might come true:

    'The virgin shall conceive and have a child, and they
    shall give him the name Emmanuel,'

for that name means, 'God is with us.' So Joseph woke
from sleep and carried out the instructions of the angel
of the Lord. He married Mary, but he did not have any
intercourse with her, until she had had her son. And he
called him by the name Jesus.

Matthew 1:18–25

O God who hast ordained that whatever is to be desired, should be sought by labour, and who, by thy blessing, bringest honest labour to good effect; look with mercy upon my studies and endeavours. Grant me, O Lord, to design only what is lawful and right; and afford me calmness of mind and steadiness of purpose, that I may so do thy will in this short life, as to obtain happiness in the world to come, for the sake of Jesus Christ our Lord.

Samuel Johnson

Tuesday: First Week

Help me, O God, like Jesus to be growing all the time.
Help me to live in such a way that I will always bring
health to my body, so that I may grow stronger and
fitter every day.
Help me in my studies to widen and deepen my mind by
learning some new thing each day, so that I may come
to think for myself and to think wisely and to think well.
Help me to live in such a way that I may bring pleasure to
those who love me, joy to you, and credit to myself;
through Jesus Christ my Lord. Amen.

THE BOY JESUS

Every year Jesus' parents used to go to Jerusalem for the
Festival of the Passover. When he was twelve years old,
they went up to the festival as they usually did. They
stayed to the very end of the festival, and, when they were
on their way back home, the boy Jesus stayed on in
Jerusalem. His parents were not aware that he had done
so. They thought that he was in the caravan, and, at the
end of the first day's journey, they began to search for him
among their relations and friends. When they did not find
him, they turned back to Jerusalem, searching for him as
they went. It was three days before they discovered him in
the Temple precincts, sitting in the middle of the teachers,
listening to them, and asking them questions. All the
isteners were amazed at his intelligence and at his
answers. They were very surprised to see him there.
'Child,' his mother said to him, 'why have you behaved
like this to us? Your father and I have been searching for
you, and we have been worried to distraction.' 'Why had
you to look for me?' he said. 'Didn't you know that I was
bound to be in my Father's house?'

They did not understand the meaning of what he said. So he went down with them, and came to Nazareth, and he was obedient to them. His mother stored all these things in her memory and kept thinking about them. And Jesus grew wiser in mind and bigger in body, and more and more he won the approval of God and of his fellow men.

Luke 2:41–52

O Holy Spirit of God,
    who with thy holy breath doth cleanse the hearts and
        minds of men,
    comforting them when they be in sorrow,
    leading them when they be out of the way,
    kindling them when they be cold,
    knitting them together when they be at variance,
    and enriching them with manifold gifts;
        by whose working all things live:
We beseech thee to maintain and daily to increase the gifts
    which thou hast vouchsafed to us;
    that with thy light before us and within us we may pass
    through this world
        without stumbling and without straying;
    who livest and reignest with the Father and the Son,
        everlastingly.

Erasmus

Wednesday: First Week

O God, bless me in every part of my life.
At home,
> help me to be thoughtful, considerate and kind.

At school,
> help me to be diligent, attentive and respectful to those who are in authority.

On the playing field,
> help me to play hard, but to play fair. Help me not to boast if I win, and not to make excuses if I lose.

On the streets,
> help me never to behave in any way which would dishonour the uniform I wear.

Make me at all times true to myself, true to my loved ones and true to you; through Jesus Christ my Lord. Amen.

THE HOUR STRIKES

When the people were in a state of expectancy, and when they were all debating in their minds whether John could be the Messiah, John said to them all: 'I baptize you with water, but the One who is stronger than I is coming. I am not fit to untie the strap of his sandals. He will baptize you with the Holy Spirit and with fire. He is going to winnow the chaff from the corn. He will cleanse every speck of rubbish from his threshing-floor, and gather the corn into his granary, but he will burn the chaff with the fire that nothing can put out.'

So, then, appealing to the people with these and many another plea, John announced the Good News to them. But, when Herod the tetrarch was reproved by him for his conduct in the matter of Herodias, his brother's wife, and for all the other wicked things he had done, in addition to all his other crimes, he shut up John in prison.

When all the people had been baptized, Jesus too was baptized, and, while he was praying, heaven was opened, and the Holy Spirit in bodily form came down like a dove on him, and there came a voice from heaven: 'You are my Son, the Beloved and Only One, on whom my favour rests.'

Luke 3:15–22

God be in my head
And in my understanding.
God be in mine eyes
And in my looking.
God be in my mouth
And in my speaking.
God be in my heart
And in my thinking.
God be at mine end
And at my departing.

Sarum Primer 1527

Thursday: First Week

O God, when I am tempted, help me to resist temptation.

> Make me resolved that I will never give those who
> love me reason to blush for anything I have done.
> Make me resolved never to do anything which would
> lower my own self-respect.
> Help me to remember that you are always there to
> give me your help in the struggle.
> Help me to live all through today in such a way that
> I will have no regrets when evening comes;
> through Jesus Christ my Lord. Amen.

JESUS AND JOHN

John's coat was made of camel's hair, and he wore a
leather belt round his waist. His food consisted of locusts
and wild honey. People from Jerusalem and from all over
Judaea and from all over the Jordan valley flocked out to
him. And a continuous stream of them were baptized in
the River Jordan, while they confessed their sins.

When John saw the Pharisees and Sadducees coming
in large numbers to be baptized, he said to them: 'Brood
of vipers! Who put it into your heads to flee from the
coming wrath? Prove the sincerity of your repentance by
your life and conduct. Don't get the idea that you can say
to yourselves: "We have Abraham as our father." For I tell
you, God can produce children for Abraham from these
stones. Even now the axe is poised at the root of the trees.
Every tree which does not produce good fruit is going to be
cut down and flung into the fire. I baptize you with water
to make you repent. He who is coming after me is stronger
than I am. I am not fit to carry his sandals. He will
baptize you with the Holy Spirit and with fire. He is going
to winnow the chaff from the corn, and he will clear every

speck of rubbish from his threshing-floor. His corn he will gather into the storehouse; the chaff he will burn with fire that nothing can put out.'

At that time Jesus came from Galilee to the Jordan to be baptized by John. John tried to stop him. 'I need to be baptized by you,' he said, 'and are you coming to me?' 'For the present,' Jesus answered, 'let it be so, for the right thing for us to do is to do everything a good man ought to do.' Then John let him have his way. No sooner had Jesus been baptized and come out of the water, than the heavens were opened, and John saw the Spirit coming down like a dove and settling on him. And there came a voice from heaven. 'This is my Son, the Beloved and Only One,' the voice said, 'and on him my favour rests.'

Matthew 3:4–17

O Lord, make thy way plain before me. Let thy glory be my end. Thy Word my rule, and then, thy will be done.
King Charles I

Friday: First Week

O God, give me the gift of perseverance.

> If I fail in something the first time, help me to try and try again, until I succeed.
> If I have to do something difficult, help me not to get discouraged, but to keep on trying.
> If I find that results are slow to come, give me patience that I may learn to wait.
> Help me to remember that the more difficult a thing is, the greater is the satisfaction in achieving it.
> Help me to welcome every difficulty as a challenge and an opportunity for victory; through Jesus Christ my Lord. Amen.

JESUS IN HIS HOME TOWN

He went to Nazareth, where he had been brought up, and, as his habit was, he went into the synagogue on the Sabbath. He rose to read the scripture lesson. The roll containing the prophecies of Isaiah was handed to him. He unrolled the roll and found the passage where it is written:

> 'The Spirit of the Lord is upon me,
> because he has anointed me,
> to bring good news to the poor.
> He has sent me to announce to the prisoners
> that they will be liberated,
> and to the blind that they will see again,
> to send away in freedom
> those who have been broken by life,
> to announce that the year
> when the favour of God will be shown has come.'

He rolled up the roll, and handed it back to the officer. He took the preacher's seat, and the eyes of everyone in the synagogue were fixed intently on him. 'Today,' he said to them, 'this passage of scripture has come true, as you listened to it.'

They all agreed that the reports that they had heard of him were true, and they were astonished at the gracious words he spoke. 'Isn't this Joseph's son?' they said. He said: 'You are bound to quote the proverb to me, "Doctor, cure yourself." Do here in your home country all that we have heard about you doing in Capernaum.' He went on: 'This is the truth I tell you, no prophet is accepted in his own native place. You know quite well that it is the fact that there was many a widow in Israel in Elijah's time, when the sky was closed for three and a half years, and there was a severe famine all over the country; but to none of them was Elijah sent; he was sent to a widow in Sarepta in Sidon. There was many a leper in Israel in the time of Elisha; and none of them was cured; but Naaman the Syrian was.' The people in the synagogue were all enraged, when they heard him speak like this. They rose from their seats and hustled him out of the town. They took him to the brow of the hill on which their town is built, to hurl him down. But he walked straight through the middle of them, and went on his way.

Luke 4:16–30

O Lord God, when thou givest to thy servants to endeavour any great matter, grant us to know that it is not the beginning but the continuing of the same, until it be thoroughly finished, which yieldeth the true glory.

Sir Francis Drake

Saturday: First Week

Today, O God, I am free from my classes and my work. Help me not to spend today in idleness, but to use it well.

> Help me to engage in some game or activity which will make me fitter in body.
>
> Help me to use today to listen to some good music, to read some good book, to see some good film or play, to broaden my mind.
>
> Help me to use today to spend some time with my friends.
>
> Help me to use part of today to do something for someone else.
>
> Help me to use today for such rest and relaxation as will enable me to work and study better in the week to come; through Jesus Christ my Lord. Amen.

JESUS AND A CENTURION

When Jesus came into Capernaum, a centurion came up to him with an urgent appeal. 'Sir,' he said, 'my servant is lying at home paralysed and in terrible pain.' 'I will come and cure him,' Jesus said. 'Sir,' answered the centurion, 'I am not fit to have you come into my house. All I ask you to do is to say the word, and my servant will be cured. For I too know what it is to be under authority, and I have soldiers under my command. I am used to saying to one, "Go" and he goes, and to another, "Come here" and he comes, and to my slave, "Do this" and he does it.' Jesus was astonished to hear this. 'I tell you truly,' he said to those who were following him, 'I have not found anyone in Israel with a faith like this. I tell you that many will come from the east and the west and will be fellow-guests with Abraham and Isaac and Jacob in the Kingdom of Heaven, but those who were born to be members of the

Kingdom will be flung out into the outer darkness, where there will be tears and agony. Go,' Jesus said to the centurion. 'Because you have a faith like this, your prayer is granted.' And the servant was cured at that very hour.

Matthew 8:5–13

O Lord Jesus Christ, who hast given thy life to redeem me, thyself for my example, thy word for my rule, thy grace for my guide, thy body on the cross for the sin of my soul: enter in and take possession of my heart, and dwell with me for ever.

After Jeremy Taylor

Sunday: First Week

O God, Sunday is the day which ought to be different from other days. Help me to make it so.

> Help me to use today to think more definitely about you.
> Help me to worship with your people today. And if I don't worship in church, help me to find a few minutes to be alone, and to see you in the beauty of the world you have made.
> On this, your day, help me to remember you.
> This I ask for your love's sake. Amen.

THE KIND OF PEOPLE JESUS WANTS

As Jesus was walking along from there, he saw a man called Matthew, sitting in the office where he collected the customs duties. 'Follow me!' he said. And Matthew rose from his seat and followed him.

Jesus was sitting at a meal in the house, and many tax-collectors and people with whom no respectable Jew would have had anything to do came to be guests along with Jesus and his disciples. When the Pharisees saw this, they said to the disciples: 'Why does your Teacher eat with tax-collectors and with people with whom no respectable Jew would have anything to do?' Jesus heard this. 'It is not those who are well who need a doctor,' he said, 'but those who are ill. Go and learn the meaning of the saying, "It is mercy I want, not sacrifice." For I did not come to bring an invitation to those who are good but to those who are sinners.'

Matthew 9:9–13

Give unto us, O Lord, we humbly beseech thee, a wise, a sober, a patient, an understanding, a devout, a religious, a courageous heart; a soul full of devotion to do thee service, strength against all temptations; through Jesus Christ our Lord. Amen.

Archbishop Laud

Monday: Second Week

Thank you, O God, for another day.
  Help me to spend it wisely and to spend it well.
Grant that everything I do today
  may be done as well as I can do it.
Grant that everyone I meet
  may be happier for the meeting.
Keep me all through today
  conscientious in my work;
  truthful in my speaking;
  loyal to my friends;
  faithful to those who love me;
  through Jesus Christ my Lord. Amen.

MARCHING ORDERS

'You must not suppose that the result of my coming will be peace for the world. The result of my coming will not be peace but a sword. My coming is bound to result in a cleavage between a man and his father, between a daughter and her mother, between a daughter-in-law and her mother-in-law. A man's enemies will be his own kith and kin.

'If a man loves his father and mother more than he loves me, he is not fit to belong to me. If a man loves his son or daughter more than he loves me, he is not fit to belong to me. If a man does not take up his cross and follow in my footsteps, he is not fit to belong to me. To find your life is to lose it, and to lose it for my sake is to find it.'

Matthew 10:34–39

O Lord Jesus Christ, who art the way, the truth, and the life, we pray thee suffer us not to stray from thee, who art the way, nor to distrust thee, who art the truth, nor to rest in any other thing than thee, who are the life. Teach us by thy Holy Spirit what to believe, what to do, and wherein to take our rest. For thine own name's sake we ask it. Amen.

Erasmus

Tuesday: Second Week

O God, make me good at learning.

Give me the concentration of mind and the retentive
memory I need to learn my lessons and my trade.
Help me to learn from advice, and to pay attention to
people who have walked the road before and
who know its pitfalls.
Help me to learn from experience and grant that I
may not make the same mistakes over again
until they become habits.

Help me each day to make myself a little better and a little wiser; through Jesus Christ my Lord. Amen.

THE ULTIMATE PROOF

When news of the things that the Messiah was doing
reached John in prison, he sent his disciples to ask him:
'Are you the One who is to come, or are we to go on
waiting and hoping for someone else?' 'Go,' answered
Jesus, 'and tell John the story of all you are hearing
and seeing. Blind men are seeing again; lame men are
walking; lepers are being cleansed; deaf men are hearing;
dead men are being raised to life; poor men are hearing
the Good News. And happy is the man who does not find
himself antagonized by me.'

Matthew 11:2–6

May God the Father bless us; may Christ take care of us;
the Holy Ghost enlighten us all the days of our life. The
Lord be our defender and keeper of body and soul, both
now and for ever, to the ages of ages. Amen.

Aedelwald

Wednesday: Second Week

O God, you have given me life. Help me to give to people what I ought to give:

   To my teachers, respect and attention;
   to my employers, diligence and honest service;
   to my parents, love and obedience;
   to my friends, loyalty and reliability;
   to everyone, friendliness and helpfulness.

Help me to give to each part of my life what I ought to give:

   To learning, concentration;
   to work, always my best effort;
   to my home, considerateness;
   to pleasure, purity;
   to love, fidelity.

Help me to live life as it ought to be lived, so that at the end I may have no regrets; through Jesus Christ my Lord. Amen.

THE RESPONSIBILITY OF PRIVILEGE

It was then that Jesus reproached the towns in which very many of his miracles had been performed, because they refused to repent. 'Tragic will be your fate, Chorazin! Tragic will be your fate, Bethsaida! For, if the miracles which have been done in you had been done in Tyre and Sidon, they would long ago have repented in sackcloth and ashes. But I tell you, Tyre and Sidon will get off more lightly in the day of judgement than you. And you, Capernaum – do you think you are going to be exalted as high as heaven? You will go down to the depths of hell. For, if the miracles which have been done in you had been done in Sodom, it would still be standing today. But I tell you, the land of Sodom will get off more lightly in the day of judgement than you!'

Matthew 11:20–24

Almighty and merciful God, the fountain of all goodness, who knowest the thoughts of our hearts, we confess unto thee that we have sinned against thee, and done evil in thy sight. Wash us, we beseech thee, from the stains of our past sins, and give us grace and power to put away all hurtful things, so that, being delivered from the bondage of sin, we may bring forth worthy fruits of repentance. O Eternal Light, shine into our hearts. O Eternal Goodness, deliver us from evil. O Eternal Power, be thou our support. Eternal Wisdom, scatter the darkness of our ignorance. Eternal Pity, have mercy upon us. Grant unto us, that with all our hearts, and minds, and strength, we may evermore seek thy face; and finally, bring us, in thine infinite mercy, to thy holy presence. So strengthen our weakness, that, following in the footsteps of thy blessed Son, we may obtain thy mercy, and enter into thy promised joy; through the same Jesus Christ, our only saviour and redeemer. Amen.

A. F. Alcuinus

Thursday: Second Week

O God, help me to conquer the things which would keep me from being what I can be, and what I ought to be:

> The inattention which makes me let things go in at one ear and out at the other;
>
> The careless workmanship which does not put its best into every job;
>
> The self-will which makes me resent and refuse guidance, and makes me take my own way – so often to trouble;
>
> The laziness which makes me do nothing when all kinds of things are needing to be done;
>
> The ingratitude which hurts those who have been kind to me;
>
> The cowardice which makes me go with the crowd because I am afraid to stand alone;
>
> The disloyalty which makes me let down my friends and disappoint those who love me –

Preserve me from all these things, O God. Strengthen me where I am weak; correct me where I am wrong; cleanse and purify me from all the faults which spoil my life; through Jesus Christ my Lord. Amen.

THE GROWTH OF OPPOSITION

'If you had known the meaning of the saying, "It is mercy I want, not sacrifice," you would not have condemned those who are blameless, for the Son of Man's authority extends over the Sabbath.'

He moved on from there, and went into their synagogue. There was a man there with a withered hand. In an attempt to find something which they could use as a charge against him, they asked him: 'Is it permitted to heal on the Sabbath day?' 'If one of you has a sheep,' he said, 'and the sheep falls into a hole in the ground on the Sabbath day, will he not take a grip of it and lift it out? Surely you will admit that a man is more valuable than a sheep? Obviously, there is no law to stop a man doing good on the Sabbath day.' Then he said to the man: 'Stretch out your hand!' He stretched it out, and it was restored, healthy as the other. The Pharisees went away and concocted a scheme to kill him.

Matthew 12:7–14

Lord Jesus, by the indwelling of thy most Holy Spirit, purge our eyes to discern and contemplate thee until we attain to see as thou seest, judge as thou judgest, choose as thou choosest, and having sought and found thee, to behold thee for ever and ever. We ask this for thy name's sake. Amen.

Christina G. Rossetti

Friday: Second Week

Forgive me, O God, for all the things for which I am sorry now:

> For things I said, which were not true, which were not pure, which were not kind;
> For things I did which were not honourable, which were not honest, which were not straight;
> For people I hurt by being thoughtless and insensitive, by being selfish and inconsiderate, by being cruel and callous and deliberately wounding;

> Forgive me, O God.

Help me from now on to keep a watch on my deeds and words so that I may never bring grief to others or sorrow to myself; through Jesus Christ my Lord. Amen.

THE SEED AND THE SOIL

On that day Jesus went out of the house and sat by the lake-side. Such crowds gathered to listen to him that he got into a boat and sat in it, while the crowd all stood on the shore. He used parables to tell them many things.

'Look!' he said. 'A sower went out to sow his seed. As he sowed, some seeds fell by the side of the road, and the birds came and snapped them up. Others fell on ground where there was only a thin skin of earth over the rock, and, because the soil was so shallow, they sprang up immediately, but when the sun rose, they were scorched, and they withered, because they had no root. Some fell among thorn-bushes, and the thorn-bushes shot up and choked the life out of them. Others fell on good ground, and produced a crop, some a hundred times, some sixty times, some thirty times as much as had been sown. If a man has ears, let him hear.'

Matthew 13:1–9

Almighty God, the giver of all good things, without whose help all labour is ineffectual, and without whose grace all wisdom is folly, grant, we beseech thee, that in all our undertakings, thy Holy Spirit may not be withheld from us: but that we may promote thy glory, and the salvation both of ourselves and others. Grant this, O Lord, for the sake of Jesus Christ our Lord. Amen.

Samuel Johnson

Saturday: Second Week

Lord Jesus, help me to have the same attitude to others as you had.

Give me a quick eye to see when others need help, and a ready hand to offer help where it is needed.

Give me a heart which is not cold but warm, a heart that is easily touched and moved at the sight of someone in sorrow or in need.

Give me the gift of sympathy so that I may never regard an appeal for help as a nuisance but rather as an opportunity.

Give me a feeling of responsibility to be a good example to those who are younger than I am. Give me respect to those who are older. And give me courtesy to everyone.

This I ask for your love's sake. Amen.

FROM SMALL BEGINNINGS

Jesus gave them another parable to think about. 'The Kingdom of Heaven,' he said, 'is like a grain of mustard seed, which a man took and sowed in his field. It is the smallest of all seeds, but when it has reached full growth, it becomes the biggest of all kitchen herbs, and grows into a tree big enough for the birds of the sky to come and nest among its branches.'

He told them another parable. 'The Kingdom of Heaven works like a piece of leaven,' he said, 'which a woman took and inserted into three pecks of flour, with the result that it was all leavened.'

Matthew 13:31–33

O Lord, lift up the light of thy countenance upon us; let thy peace rule in our hearts, and may it be our strength and our song, in the house of our pilgrimage. We commit ourselves to thy care and keeping this day; let thy grace be mighty in us, and sufficient for us, and let it work in us both to will and to do of thine own good pleasure, and grant us strength for all the duties of the day. Keep us from sin. Give us the rule over our own spirits, and keep us from speaking unadvisedly with our lips. May we live together in peace and holy love, and do thou command thy blessing upon us, even life for ever more. Prepare us for all the events of the day, for we know not what a day may bring forth. Give us grace to deny ourselves; to take up our cross daily, and to follow in the steps of our Lord and master, Jesus Christ our Lord. Amen.

Matthew Henry

Sunday: Second Week

O God, I thank you that you have made me as I am.

> I thank you for a healthy body. Help me never to develop habits or to indulge in pleasures which would make me physically less fit.
>
> I thank you for a healthy mind. Help me to use it to keep learning things, and to think until I reach an answer to my problems.
>
> I thank you for all the interest of life, that there are always new things to do and to see.
>
> I thank you for the people who mean much to me – my friends, my teachers, my father and mother. Help me to live so that I will never disappoint them; through Jesus Christ my Lord. Amen.

GOD'S PLENTY

When he disembarked, he saw a great crowd, and he was heart-sorry for them, and cured their sick. Late on in the day the disciples came to him. 'This place is a desert,' they said, 'and it is now past the time for the evening meal. Send the crowd away into the villages to buy themselves food.' 'There is no necessity for them to go away,' Jesus said. 'You must give them something to eat.' 'All that we have here,' they said to him, 'is five loaves and two fishes.' 'Bring them to me,' Jesus said. So he ordered the crowd to sit down on the grass. He took the five loaves and the two fishes. He looked up to heaven and said the blessing. He broke the loaves into pieces and gave them to the disciples, and the disciples gave them to the crowds. They all ate until they could eat no more. They collected twelve basketfuls of pieces of bread that were left over. Those who ate numbered about five thousand men, not counting women and children.

Matthew 14:14–21

We beseech thee, O Lord, in thy loving-kindness, to pour thy holy light into our souls; that we may ever be devoted to thee, by whose wisdom we were created, and by whose providence we are governed; through Jesus Christ our Lord. Amen.

Gelasian Sacramentary

Monday: Third Week

O God, bless all the people for whom life is hard and
    difficult.
Those who are ill and who must lie in bed at home or in
    hospital;
Those who cannot walk or run or jump and play games;
Those who are lonely because they are away from home;
Those who are sad because someone they loved has died;
Those who are not very clever and for whom it is a struggle
    to keep up with the rest of the class;
Those who are shy and who find it difficult to meet people;
Those who are poor and who never have enough.

Help me, O God, to remember all such people, and to do
    all I can to help them; through Jesus Christ my Lord.
    Amen.

JESUS AND A CANAANITE

Jesus left there and withdrew to the districts of Tyre and
Sidon. A Canaanite woman from these parts came to him.
'Take pity on me, sir, Son of David,' she kept shouting. 'My
daughter is possessed by a demon and is very ill.' Jesus did
not answer her at all. His disciples came and asked him:
'Send her away. She won't stop following us and shouting
at us.' Jesus said: 'It is only to the lost sheep of the family
of Israel that I have been sent.' She came and knelt in front
of him in entreaty. 'Sir,' she said, 'help me.' 'It is not
proper,' Jesus answered, 'to take the bread which belongs
to the children and to fling it to the pet dogs.' 'True, sir,'
she said, 'but the pet dogs do eat their share of the crumbs
which fall from their master's table.' At that Jesus
answered: 'You have great faith. Let your wish be
granted.' From that moment her daughter was cured.

Matthew 15:21–28

From the unreal lead me to the real;
from darkness lead me to light;
from death lead me to deathlessness.

Ancient Indian Prayer

Tuesday: Third Week

O God, keep me from the things which would spoil life for myself and for others.

Keep me from procrastination, from putting things off until tomorrow. Whatever I have to do, help me to do it now, in case it is too late to do it at all.

Save me from the quick temper which would make me do and say things for which I would afterwards be very sorry.

Save me from the disobliging spirit, and when I am asked to do anything, help me to do it at once and to do it with a good grace.

Save me from being envious and discontented.

Help me to do the best I can with the things I have and with myself as I am.

Save me from being moody and irritable, and help me to meet life with a smile; through Jesus Christ my Lord. Amen.

THE GREAT RECOGNITION

When Jesus had come to the districts of Caesarea Philippi, he put a question to his disciples. 'Who are people saying that the Son of Man is?' he asked. They said: 'Some are saying, John the Baptizer; others, Elijah; others, Jeremiah, or one of the prophets.' 'And you,' he said to them, 'who do you say that I am?' Simon Peter answered: 'You are the Messiah, the Son of the living God!' 'You are indeed blessed, Simon Barjona,' Jesus said, 'for it was no human being who revealed this to you; it was my Father who is in heaven. I tell you, you are Peter – the man whose name means a rock – and on this rock I will erect my Church, and the powers of death will be helpless to harm it. I will give you the keys of the Kingdom of Heaven, and whatever you

forbid on earth will be forbidden in heaven, and whatever
you allow on earth will be allowed in heaven.' Jesus gave
strict orders to his disciples not to tell anyone that he was
the Messiah.

Matthew 16:13–20

O God, who by thy Spirit in our hearts dost lead men to
desire thy perfection, to seek for truths and to rejoice in
beauty: illuminate and inspire, we beseech thee, all
thinkers, writers, artists and craftsmen; that, in whatsoever is true and pure and lovely, thy name may be
hallowed and thy kingdom come on earth; through Jesus
Christ our Lord.

Prayer found in St Anselm's Chapel, Canterbury

Wednesday: Third Week

O God, bless our country.

Bless those who are in Parliament, in the Cabinet; those who serve as permanent officials in the departments of state.

Grant that they may have no unworthy ambitions in which they are out for their own glory and their own profit; but grant that their ambition may be to make this a Christian country, in which people shall walk in the freedom of truth and the light of knowledge, a country in which none shall have too little and none too much.

Help me to be a good citizen of my country, doing an honest day's work, willing some day to take my part in the government of my city, my town, my district, my region.

Save me from being one of the many people who take everything and who give nothing.

Make me grateful for all that I have received, and determined to hand it on still better; through Jesus Christ my Lord. Amen.

ON LOSING AND SAVING ONE'S SOUL

Jesus went on to say to his disciples: 'If anyone wishes to walk in my steps, he must once and for all say No to himself; he must decide to take up his cross, and he must keep on following me. Anyone who wishes to keep his life safe will lose it, but anyone who is prepared to lose his life for my sake will find it. What good will it do to a man to gain the whole world, if in so doing he forfeits his own life? What could a man give that would be an equal exchange for his life? For the Son of Man will come with his angels in his Father's glory, and he will settle accounts with each man on the basis of how each man has lived. I tell you truly, there are some of those who are standing here who will not experience death until they see the Son of Man coming in his Kingdom.'

Matthew 16:24–28

We commend unto thee, O Lord,
    our souls and our bodies,
    our minds and our thoughts,
    our prayers and our hopes,
    our health and our work,
    our life and our death,
    our parents and brothers and sisters,
    our benefactors and friends,
    our neighbours, our countrymen,
        and all Christian folk
            this day and always.
                Lancelot Andrewes

Thursday: Third Week

Help me, O God, to try to make the work of other people easier and not harder.

At home, help me to be careful and tidy, cheerful and willing to take my share of the household chores.

At school, help me to behave well, and to work and study conscientiously.

At games, grant that I may never be guilty of any unfair action; grant that I would rather lose than win by a foul.

Where there are rules and regulations, help me to keep them and not to cause trouble by breaking them; through Jesus Christ my Lord. Amen.

THE TRANSFIGURATION

About a week later Jesus took with him Peter and James and John, James's brother, and brought them up into a high mountain alone. He was transformed before their very eyes. His face shone like the sun, and his clothes became as white as the light. Moses and Elijah appeared to them, talking to Jesus. 'Master,' Peter said to Jesus, 'it is a wonderful thing for us to be here. Would you like me to make three shelters here, one for you, one for Moses, and one for Elijah?' While he was still speaking, a shining cloud enveloped them, and out of the cloud a voice said: 'This is my Son, the Beloved and Only One, on whom my favour rests. Listen to him!' When the disciples heard this, they flung themselves face down on the ground, for they were terrified. Jesus came and touched them. 'Up!' he said. 'Don't be afraid!' And when they looked up, the only person they could see was Jesus, all by himself.

Matthew 17:1–8

O thou almighty will
Faint are thy children, till
    Thou come with power:
Strength of our good intents,
In our frail home, defence,
Calm of faith's confidence,
    Come, in this hour!

O thou most tender love!
Deep in our spirits move:
    Tarry, dear guest!
Quench thou our passion's fire,
Raise thou each low desire,
Deeds of brave love inspire,
    Quickener and rest!

O light serene and still!
Come, and our spirit fill,
    Bring in the day:
Guide of our feeble sight,
Star of our darkest night,
Shine on the path of right,
    Show us the way!
                King Robert of France

Friday: Third Week

Help me, O God, to banish self from life:

> The selfishness which makes me the centre of the
> whole universe;
> The self-conceit which thinks far too highly of itself;
> The self-will which resents and refuses all advice;
> The self-pity which is sorry for itself;
> The self-deception which refuses to see itself as it is;
> The self-abasement which is only an excuse to shirk
> my duties and my responsibilities;
> The self-excusing which always puts the blame on
> someone else;

Help me to be done with all these; through Jesus Christ my
Lord. Amen.

JESUS AND THE EPILEPTIC BOY

When they reached the crowd, a man came to Jesus and
knelt at his feet. 'Sir,' he said, 'take pity on my son. He is
an epileptic, and he is very ill. He often falls into the fire
and into the water. And I brought him to your disciples,
and they were quite unable to cure him.' 'This modern
generation has no faith,' Jesus answered. 'There is a fatal
perversity about it. How long have I to be with you? How
long must I endure you? Bring him here to me!' Then Jesus
spoke to him with a stern authority, and the demon came
out of him, and there and then the boy was cured. Afterwards when they were alone, the disciples came to Jesus.
'Why were we unable to eject the demon?' they asked him.
'Because,' he said, 'you have so little faith. I tell you truly,
if you have faith as big as a mustard seed, you will say to
this mountain: "Move from here to there," and it will
remove itself. There will be nothing you cannot do.'

Lord, give us to go blithely on our business all this day, bring us to our resting beds weary and content and un-dishonoured, and grant us in the end the gift of sleep.

Robert Louis Stevenson

O God, who has folded back the mantle of the night, to clothe us in the golden glory of the day, chase from our hearts all gloomy thoughts, and make us glad with the brightness of hope, that we may effectively aspire to unwon virtues; through Jesus Christ our Lord.

Ancient Collect

Saturday: Third Week

O God, this is Saturday, the day when I don't need to go
out to school or to work. It is the day when I can do
what I like. Help me to make good use of it.

Help me to use it for rest, without being lazy.
If I use it to play games, help me to play hard but to
play clean.
If I use it to spectate, help me to enjoy it, and to support my team without being a fanatic about it.
If I go to the cinema or to the theatre, or if I listen to
music or go dancing, help me to enjoy it to the
full and to remain well-behaved.
Help me to use this Saturday to be refreshed in body
and stimulated in mind; through Jesus Christ my
Lord. Amen.

FORGIVE TO BE FORGIVEN

Peter came to Jesus. 'Master,' he said to him, 'how often
ought I to forgive my fellow man, if he goes on wronging
me? As many as seven times?' 'I tell you,' Jesus said to
him, 'not as many as seven times, but as many as seven-
ty times seven. That is why what happens in the Kingdom
of Heaven can be compared with the situation which
arose when a king wished to settle accounts with his servants. When he began to settle up, one debtor was
brought in who owed him two and a half million pounds.
He was quite unable to pay. So his master gave orders for
him to be sold, along with his wife and children and everything he had, and the money to be paid over. The servant
threw himself on his knees at his master's feet. "Give me
time," he said, "and I will pay you everything in full." The
servant's master was heart-sorry for the man, and let him
go free, and remitted the debt. That same servant went out

and met one of his fellow-servants who owed him five pounds. He seized him by the throat. "Pay your debt!" he said. His fellow-servant threw himself at his feet. "Give me time," he begged, "and I will pay you in full." He refused, and went and had him thrown into prison, until he should pay the debt in full. When his fellow-servants saw what had happened, they were very distressed. So they went to their master and informed him of all that had happened. The master sent for the servant. "You utter scoundrel!" he said. "I remitted that whole debt of yours, because you pleaded with me to do so. Surely you should have had the same pity for your fellow-servant as I had for you." The master was furious, and handed him over to the torturers until he should repay the whole debt in full. My heavenly Father will do the same to you, if you do not, each one of you, genuinely forgive your fellow man.'

Matthew 18:21–35

O Lord God Almighty, I charge thee of thy great mercy and by the token of thy holy rood that thou guide me to thy will and to my soul's need better than I can myself, that above all things I may inwardly love thee with a clear mind and clean body; for thou art my maker, my help and my hope.

King Alfred The Great

Sunday: Third Week

O God, help me to remember that this is the Lord's Day,
   and help me to remember that it is called that
   because it is the day on which Jesus rose from the
   dead.
So help me to remember that Jesus is not just a person
   in a book, but that he is here always although we
   cannot see him. He is here to warn us in any time of
   temptation and to help us in any time of difficulty.
Help us to remember that he is the unseen companion of
   all my way, and the unseen guest in every home.
This I ask for your love's sake. Amen.

THE ONE THING LACKING

A man came to Jesus. 'Teacher,' he said, 'what must I do
to make myself good enough to possess eternal life?' 'Why
do you ask me about what is good?' Jesus said to him. 'One
and One alone is good. If you want to get into life, obey
the commandments.' 'What commandments?' he said.
Jesus said: 'The commandments which say: You must not
kill, You must not commit adultery, You must not steal,
You must not tell lies about anyone, Honour your father
and your mother, and, You must love your neighbour as
yourself.' 'I have obeyed all these,' the young man said to
him. 'What is still missing in me?' 'If you really want to be
perfect,' Jesus said to him, 'go and sell everything you
have and give the proceeds to the poor, and you will have
treasure in heaven. Then come! Follow me!' When the
young man heard Jesus say this, he went sadly away, for
he was very wealthy.

Matthew 19:16–22

Merciful God, be thou now unto us a strong tower of defence. Give us grace to await thy leisure, and patiently to bear what thou doest unto us, nothing doubting thy goodness towards us. Therefore do with us in all things as thou wilt: Only arm us, we beseech thee, with thy armour, that we may stand fast; above all things taking to us the shield of faith, praying always that we may refer ourselves wholly to thy will, being assuredly persuaded that all thou doest cannot but be well. And unto thee be all honour and glory.

Lady Jane Grey

Monday: Fourth Week

O God, it is back to work and back to study today.

Whatever I have to do, help me to put my best into it. Even
   when work is dull, help me to do it well, always
   remembering that to do today's work well is to be on
   the way to more interesting work tomorrow.

Help me to remember that there is no easy way to the top,
   and that I will only get there by doing each day's work
   as well as it can be done, whatever it may be; through
   Jesus Christ my Lord. Amen.

MASTER OR SERVANT? WHICH IS YOUR AMBITION?

It was then the mother of Zebedee's sons came to him with
her sons. She knelt before him and asked him to give her
a special favour. 'What is it you want?' he said to her. 'I
want my two sons,' she said, 'to sit one on your right hand
and one on your left in your Kingdom.' 'You do not know
what you are asking for,' Jesus said. 'Can you pass
through the bitter experience through which I must pass?'
'We can,' they said. He said to them: 'You will pass
through the same experience as I must go through, but to
sit on my right hand and on my left is not in my power to
give you. That is reserved for those for whom it has been
prepared by my Father.'

   When the ten heard about this, they were annoyed
with the two brothers. Jesus called them to him. 'You
know,' he said, 'that the leaders of the Gentiles lord it over
them, and that in their society the mark of greatness is the
exercise of authority. But in your society the situation is
very different. With you, if anyone wishes to be great, he
must be your servant; and with you, if anyone wishes to
hold the first place, he must be everyone's slave, just as the

Son of Man did not come to be served but to serve, and to give his life as a ransom for many.'

Matthew 20:20–28

O Lord, make thy way plain before me. Let thy glory be my end. Thy word my rule, and then, thy will be done.

King Charles I

Tuesday: Fourth Week

O God, keep me from being difficult to live with.

> Keep me from being irritable, and from losing my temper about trifles.
>
> Keep me from being moody and unpredictable.
>
> Keep me from being far too critical of others, and of what they do for me.
>
> Keep me from being so self-centred that I cannot see that anyone else can ever be right.
>
> Keep me from being rude and impolite, and help me at all times to be courteous in manner and in speech.
>
> Help me always to do and be to others what I would wish them to do and be to me; through Jesus Christ my Lord. Amen.

SIGHT FOR FAITH

They were leaving Jericho followed by a large crowd. There were two blind men sitting at the roadside. When they heard that Jesus was passing, they shouted: 'Master! Take pity on us! Son of David!' The crowd sharply told them to be quiet, but they shouted all the louder: 'Master! Take pity on us! Son of David!' Jesus stopped and called them. 'What do you want me to do for you?' he said. 'Sir,' they said to him, 'the only thing we want is to be able to see.' Jesus was heart-sorry for them. He touched their eyes, and there and then their sight returned, and they followed him.

Matthew 20:29–34

Keep me, O Lord, while I tarry on this earth, in a daily serious seeking after thee, and in a believing affectionate walking with thee; that, when thou comest, I may be found not hiding my talent, nor serving my flesh, nor yet asleep with my lamp unfurnished; but waiting and longing for my Lord, my glorious God, for ever and ever.

Richard Baxter

Wednesday: Fourth Week

O God, help me to find my pleasure in the right things and in the right way.

Grant that I may never look for pleasure in anything that would make my body less fit, my mind less efficient, or my heart less pure.

Grant that I may never look for pleasure in anything which would damage things or injure people.

Grant that I may never look for pleasure in things which would lead others astray or make it easier for them to go wrong.

Grant that I may never look for pleasure in things which would afterwards bring regret or make me sorry.

Help me always to find pleasure in things which hurt no one and which bring no regrets to follow; through Jesus Christ my Lord. Amen.

THE TRIUMPHAL ENTRY

When they were near Jerusalem, and when they had reached Bethphage, at the Hill of Olives, Jesus sent on two of his disciples. 'Go into the village opposite you,' he said, 'and you will at once find a tethered donkey, and a foal with her. Untie them and bring them to me. If anyone says anything to you, you will say: "The Master needs them," and he will send them at once.' This happened so that the statement made through the prophet might come true:

> 'Say to the daughter of Sion:
> "Look! Your king is coming to you,
> gentle, and riding on an ass,
> and on a colt, the foal of a beast of burden."'

The disciples went off and carried out Jesus' instructions. They brought the donkey and the foal. They put their cloaks on them and Jesus mounted them. The huge crowd spread their cloaks on the road, while others cut down branches from the trees, and spread them on the road. The crowds who were going on ahead and the crowds who were following behind kept shouting:

'God save David's Son!
God bless him who comes in the name of the Lord!
O send your salvation from the heights of heaven!'

When Jesus entered Jerusalem, the whole city seethed with excitement. 'Who is this?' they said. The crowds said: 'This is the prophet Jesus from Nazareth in Galilee.'

Matthew 21:1–11

Accept, O Lord God, our Father, the sacrifices of our thanksgiving; this, of praise, for thy great mercies already afforded to us; and this, of prayer, for the continuance and enlargement of them; this, of penitence, for such only recompense as our sinful nature can endeavour; and this, of the love of our hearts, as the only gift thou dost ask or desire; and all these, through the all-holy and atoning sacrifice of Jesus Christ thy Son, our saviour.

John Donne

Thursday: Fourth Week

Lord Jesus, give me the things I need to live life well:

> Encouragement, when I feel that nothing is happening and that I am not getting anywhere;
>
> Resistance power, when I feel the fascination of the wrong things;
>
> The ability to stand up for what I believe is right, even if it means unpopularity and standing alone;
>
> Perseverance, especially at the times when it would be easier to give up than to go on;
>
> Honesty, that I may value truth above all things;
>
> Self-respect, so that I may never lower myself to being less than my best;

Grant me these things, God; through Jesus Christ my Lord. Amen.

THE CLEANSING OF THE TEMPLE

Jesus went into the Temple precincts, and drove out all who were selling and buying there, and upset the tables of the money-changers, and the seats of the pigeon-sellers. 'Scripture says,' he said to them, '"My house must be regarded as a house of prayer," but you are making it a brigands' den.'

The blind and the lame came to him in the Temple precincts and he cured them. When the chief priests and the experts in the Law saw the astonishing things that Jesus did, and when they heard the children shouting in the Temple precincts: 'God save David's Son!' they were enraged. 'Do you hear what the children are saying?' they said to him. 'I do,' Jesus said to them. 'Have you never read: "Out of the mouths of babes and sucklings you have brought perfect praise"?' So he left there, and went out of the city to Bethany, and spent the night there.

Matthew 21:12–17

Relieve and comfort, O Lord, all the persecuted and afflicted; speak peace to troubled consciences; strengthen the weak; confirm the strong; instruct the ignorant; deliver the oppressed from him that spoileth him; and relieve the needy that hath no helper; and bring us all, by the waters of comfort and in the ways of righteousness, to the kingdom of rest and glory; through Jesus Christ our Lord. Amen.

Bishop Jeremy Taylor

Friday: Fourth Week

O God, there is so much for which I ought to give thanks.

> For life, and life in this beautiful and interesting world;
>
> For parents and for a home and for all that is daily done for me;
>
> For school and for teachers, for work to do, for all that equips me some day to earn a living for myself and for those who will be dependent on me;
>
> For all happy and healthy pleasures which exercise my body and refresh my mind;
>
> For the loyalty of friends, for the care of loved ones, and for your love to me in Jesus who lived and died for me:
>
> I thank you.
>
> Accept my prayer through Jesus Christ my Lord. Amen.

THE HEART

'Listen to another parable. There was a householder who planted a vineyard. He surrounded it with a hedge, and dug out a pit in which the juice could be extracted from the grapes, and built a watch-tower. He then let it out to tenants and went abroad. When the fruit season arrived, he sent his servants to the tenants to receive his due share of the crop. The tenants took the servants, and beat one up, and killed another, and stoned another. Again he sent other servants, more than the first lot he had sent, and they treated them in the same way. He then sent his son to them. "They will treat my son with respect," he said. But, when the tenants saw the son, they said to themselves: "This is the heir. Come on! Let's kill him! And let us seize his estate!" So they took him, and threw him out of

the vineyard and killed him. When the owner of the vineyard comes, what will he do to these tenants?' They said,
'He will see to it that these bad men come to a bad end,
and he will let out the vineyard to other tenants, who will
pay him his full share of the crops when it is due.' Jesus
said to them: 'Have you never read in the scriptures:

"The stone which the builders rejected,
this has become the headstone of the corner.
This is the action of God,
and it is marvellous in our eyes"?

I tell you, that is why the Kingdom of God will be taken
from you, and given to a nation whose conduct befits it.'
Matthew 21:33–43

Glory be to thee, O Heavenly Father, for our being and
preservation, health and strength, understanding and
memory, friends and benefactors, and for all our abilities
of mind and body. Glory be to thee for our competent liveli-
hood, for the advantages of our education, for all known
and unobserved deliverances, and for the guard which thy
holy angels keep over us. Glory be to thee, O Lord, O
Blessed Saviour, for those ordinary gifts by which sincere
Christians have in all ages been enabled to work for their
salvation, for all the spiritual strength and support, comfort and illumination which we receive from thee, and for
all thy preserving, restraining, and sanctifying grace.
Bishop Thomas Ken

Saturday: Fourth Week

Save me from being altogether selfish in my prayers, and
help me to remember others who are in trouble.

> The sick and those who must lie in bed throughout the
> sunlit hours, especially young folk laid aside too
> soon in the morning of their day;
> Those who are sad and sorry because someone they
> loved has died;
> Those who are disappointed because something they
> wanted very much has passed them by;
> The discontented, those who live with a chip on their
> shoulder, who are their own worst enemies;
> Those who have done something wrong and who are
> in disgrace, that they may redeem themselves;
> Those who are underrated and undervalued, and
> who have never been appreciated as they ought
> to have been;
> Those who have been passed over for some office they
> had expected to receive;
> All those in pain, in sorrow, in misfortune, in dis-
> grace:

Bless all such. For your love's sake I ask it. Amen.

THE GUEST AND THE GARMENT

Once again Jesus spoke to them in parables. 'The
situation in the Kingdom of Heaven,' he said, 'is like the
situation which arose when a king gave a wedding
banquet for his son. He sent out his servants to tell the
guests, who had already received their invitations to the
banquet, to come, and they refused to come. He sent
out a second lot of servants. "Tell those who have been
invited," he said, "that I have completed the preparations

for the dinner I am giving. My oxen and specially fattened calves have been killed. Everything is ready. Come to the wedding banquet." They completely disregarded the invitation, and went off, one to his farm and another to his business. The others seized the servants, and wantonly ill-treated them, and killed them. The king was furious and sent his troops and wiped out those murderers, and burned their town. Then he said to the servants: "The wedding banquet is all ready, but those who received invitations to it did not deserve them. Go out to the open roads and invite everyone you meet to the banquet." So the servants went out to the roads and collected everyone they met, good and bad alike, and so the room where the wedding banquet was to be held was filled with guests.

'When the king came in to look at the guests, he saw a man there who was not dressed in wedding clothes. "Friend," he said to him, "why have you come like this, without wedding clothes?" The man had nothing to say. Then the king said to the attendants: "Tie him up, hand and foot, and fling him out into the outer darkness." There will be tears and agony there. For many are invited but few are chosen.'

Matthew 22:1–14

Write thy blessed name, O Lord, upon my heart, there to remain so indelibly engraved, that no prosperity, no adversity shall ever move me from thy love. Be thou to me a strong tower of defence, a comforter in tribulation, a deliverer in distress, a very present help in trouble, and a guide to heaven through the many temptations and dangers of this life.

Thomas à Kempis

Sunday: Fourth Week

Lord Jesus, this is your day. Help me to use at least some part of it to think of you.

> Help me to remember that there are other things in life than material things, and that all the material things in the world cannot make me happy if I am not right myself.
>
> Help me to remember that this is not the only world, and help me to live well in this world that I am prepared for the world to come.
>
> Help me to remember that the things which are seen are temporary and passing, but the unseen things are eternal and last for ever.
>
> So grant that I may live as always in the shadow of eternity remembering that there is a day of judgement, and that there is another world, and that what I do here will determine what life in that other world will be; through Jesus Christ my Lord. Amen.

CAESAR'S AND GOD'S

The Pharisees went and concocted a scheme to lay a verbal trap for Jesus. They sent their disciples to him along with Herod's supporters. 'Teacher,' they said to him, 'we know that you speak the truth, and that you really do teach the life that God wishes us to live. We know that it makes no difference to you who or what anyone is, and that man-made prestige means nothing to you. Well, then, tell us, what is your opinion – is it right for us to pay the poll-tax to Caesar, or is it not?' Jesus was well aware of their malicious motives. 'You are not out for information,' he said to them, 'you are out to make trouble in your two-faced maliciousness. Show me the coin with which the poll-tax is paid.' They brought him a silver piece. 'Whose portrait and whose inscription is this?' he asked. 'Caesar's,' they said. 'Well, then,' he said to them, 'pay to Caesar what belongs to Caesar, and to God what belongs to God.' When they heard that answer, they were astonished, and went away and left him.

Matthew 22:15–22

In confidence of thy goodness and great mercy, O Lord, I draw near unto thee, as a sick person to the healer, as one hungry and thirsty to the fountain of life, a creature to the creator, a desolate soul to my own tender comforter. Behold, in thee is all whatsoever I can or ought to desire; thou art my salvation and my redemption, my help and my strength. Rejoice therefore this day the soul of thy servant; for unto thee, O Lord, have I lifted up my soul.

Thomas à Kempis

Monday: Fifth Week

O God, bless and help all those who have to face life with some handicap.

Those who are lame and crippled, who cannot run and jump and play the games which other people play;

Those who are blind and who cannot see the light of the sun or the faces of their friends;

Those who are deaf, who cannot hear the voices of their friends, who cannot listen to music or the singing of the birds;

Those whose minds are disturbed and for whom the kindly light of reason burns dim;

Those who find learning difficult, and for whom it is a constant struggle to keep up with the class.

Give courage and strength and help to all those who are handicapped, and grant that those who are strong may be ever ready and willing to help them; through Jesus Christ our Lord. Amen.

THE FIRST AND GREAT COMMANDMENT

When the Pharisees heard that Jesus had silenced the Sadducees, they came in a body. One of them, a legal expert, put a question to Jesus as a test. 'Teacher,' he said, 'which is the greatest commandment in the Law?' Jesus said to him: 'You must love the Lord your God with your whole heart and your whole soul and your whole mind. This is the first and greatest commandment. And there is a second one like it: You must love your neighbour as yourself. On these two commandments the whole message of the Law and of the Prophets depends.'

Matthew 22:34–40

O living Christ, make us conscious now of thy healing nearness. Touch our eyes that we may see thee; open our ears that we may hear thy voice; enter our hearts that we may know thy love. Overshadow our souls and bodies with thy presence, that we may partake of thy strength, thy love and thy healing life.

H. C. Robbins

Tuesday: Fifth Week

Lord Jesus, I thank you for the life you lived:
> That you were born into an ordinary home;
> That you did an ordinary job, when you were the
> village carpenter of Nazareth;
> That you were tempted to sin as all men are tempted,
> and that you never fell to temptation;
> That you loved the open air, and the flowers and the
> birds, and the waters of the lake, and all people.

Lord Jesus, I thank you for the death you died:
> That you loved everyone to the bitter end;
> That you endured the worst that people could do to
> you, and still forgave them;
> That your death was for me and my salvation.

Lord Jesus, we thank you for your resurrection:
> We thank you that you rose from the dead and that
> you are alive for ever more to be the continual
> companion of our way.

Hear this our thanksgiving for your love's sake. Amen.

ALAS FOR YOU!

'Tragic will be the fate of you experts in the Law and you
Pharisees with your façade of ostentatious piety! You
roam sea and land to make one convert, and, when he has
become a convert, you make him twice as much hell-
begotten as yourselves.

'Tragic will be your fate, for you are blind guides! You
say: "If a man swears by the Temple, there is no necessity
to keep the oath, but, if a man swears by the gold of the
Temple, he is bound to keep it." You are senseless and
blind! Which is greater – the gold, or the Temple which

makes the gold sacred? You say: "If a man swears by the altar, there is no necessity to keep the oath, but, if a man swears by the gift that is on it, he is bound to keep it." You are blind! Which is greater – the gift, or the altar which makes the gift sacred? If a man swears by the altar, he swears by it and by all that is on it. If a man swears by the Temple, he swears by it, and by him whose home it is. If a man swears by heaven, he swears by the throne of God, and by him who sits on it.

'Tragic will be the fate of you experts in the Law and you Pharisees with your façade of ostentatious piety! For you meticulously pay the tenth part of your crop of mint and dill and cummin to the Temple, and you completely neglect the more important demands of the Law – justice, mercy and loyalty. You ought to have kept the second without neglecting the first. You are blind guides, you who carefully filter a midge out of your drink and then swallow a camel!

'Tragic will be the fate of you experts in the Law and you Pharisees with your façade of ostentatious piety! For you carefully clean the outside of the cup and the plate while you leave the inside full to overflowing with greed and unbridled self-indulgence. You blind Pharisee! First clean the inside of the cup, and then outside and inside will both be clean.'

Matthew 23:13–26

We thank thee, O Lord, for all who have chosen poverty or solitude for thy sake, for men of prayer, for saints in common life who have borne suffering for noble ends, and for those who have endured pain with patience and purity of life, in the strength of him who for the joy that was set before him endured the cross, ever Jesus Christ our Lord.

Anon

Wednesday: Fifth Week

Save us, O God, from the folly of putting things off until
    tomorrow or to some more distant date.
Save us from dodging the tasks we don't want to do.
Save us from shirking the things which are difficult to do.
Save us from putting things off that we are just too lazy
    to do.
Save us from putting things off because we think that we
    have plenty of time, and help us always to remember
    that tomorrow may never come for us.

Help us to remember that all we do possess is the present
    moment and that tomorrow is the most dangerous
    word in the language.
Help us to remember now our creator in the days of our
    youth, and to do things now; through Jesus Christ our
    Lord. Amen.

ALAS FOR YOU!

'Tragic will be the fate of you experts in the Law and you
Pharisees with your façade of ostentatious piety! For you
are like white-washed tombs, which look beautiful from
the outside, but which are full of dead men's bones and all
kinds of filth. So you too, as far as external appearances
go, seem to people to be carefully obeying the Law, but
you are really putting on an act, for inside you are full of
disobedience to the Law.

'Tragic will be the fate of you experts in the Law and
you Pharisees with your façade of ostentatious piety! You
build tombs for the prophets and erect lovely memorials to
good men, and you say: "If we had lived in the days of our
ancestors, we would not have been partners with them in
the murder of the prophets." By your very statement you
provide evidence that you yourselves are the descendants

of those who killed the prophets. Carry on! Equal your fathers in their sins! You serpents! You brood of vipers! How can you escape being condemned to hell?

'Let me tell you why I send you prophets and sages and experts in the Law. Some of them you will kill and crucify. Some of them you will flog in your synagogues, and hunt from town to town. The reason is that there may rest on you the responsibility for the murder of every good man from the murder of the good Abel to the murder of Zachariah, Barachiah's son, between the Temple and the altar. I tell you, retribution for all this will descend upon the people of today.

'O Jerusalem, Jerusalem! Killer of the prophets! Stoner of those who were sent to you by God! How often I have wanted to gather your children together as a bird gathers her nestlings under the shelter of her wings – and you refused! God no longer has his home among you, for, I tell you, you will not see me again until you say: "God bless him who comes as the representative of the Lord."'

Matthew 23:27–39

Give me, O Lord, a steadfast heart, which no unworthy affection may drag downwards; give me an unconquered heart, which no tribulation can wear out; give me an upright heart, which no unworthy purpose may tempt aside. Bestow upon me also, O Lord my God, understanding to know thee, wisdom to find thee, and a faithfulness that may finally embrace thee.

Thomas Aquinas

Thursday: Fifth Week

O God, help me to love my neighbour as I love myself.
Help me never to bear grudges, but to put them out of my
   mind and to forget.
Help me never to look for revenge, because looking for
   revenge leads only to more trouble.
Help me always to love others, never to seek anything but
   their good, never to try to injure anyone but always
   to help. Even if I don't like a person, help me still to
   seek nothing but his or her good.
Help me to take Jesus as my example and to go about like
   him, doing good.
This I ask for your love's sake. Amen.

TOO LATE!

'What will happen in the Kingdom of Heaven is like what
happened to ten bridesmaids, who took their lamps and
went out to meet the bridegroom. Five of them were
foolish and five were sensible. The foolish ones brought
their lamps, but they did not bring any oil with them. The
sensible ones took oil in jars along with their lamps. When
the bridegroom was a long time in coming, they grew
drowsy. They were all asleep, when in the middle of the
night there was a shout:

"Here comes the bridegroom! Out you go and meet
him!" At this all the girls woke up and trimmed their
lamps. The foolish ones said to the sensible ones: "Our
lamps have gone out. Give us some of your oil." "We can't
do that," the sensible ones answered, "because then there
might not be enough oil for us and for you. You had
better go to those who sell oil, and buy some for yourselves." While they were away buying it, the bridegroom
arrived. The bridesmaids who were ready went in to the
banquet with him, and the door was shut. Later on the

other girls arrived. "Sir!" they said, "Sir! Open the door for us!" "I tell you truly," he said, "I don't know who you are!" So, then, be sleeplessly on the watch, because you do not know the day or the hour.'

Matthew 25:1–13

Lord make me an instrument of thy peace.
Where there is hatred, let me sow love;
Where there is injury, pardon;
Where there is doubt, faith;
Where there is despair, hope;
Where there is darkness, light;
Where there is sadness, joy.

O Divine Master, grant that
I may not so much seek
To be consoled, as to console;
Not so much seek to be understood as
To understand;
Not so much seek to be
Loved as to love:
For it is in giving that we receive;
It is in pardoning, that we are pardoned;
It is in dying, that we awaken to eternal life.

St Francis of Assisi

Friday: Fifth Week

Help me, O God, to sow in my life all the fruit of the Spirit:

Love, that I may live at peace with all men;
Joy, that I may be as happy as the day is long;
Peace, that I may never be worried and anxious;
Patience, that I may learn to wait upon events and to bear with people;
Gentleness, that I may always be kind;
Goodness, that I may be an example to all;
Fidelity, that I may always keep my promise and my word;
Meekness, that I may have every passion under strict control;
Self-control, that I may be master of myself and so be fit to serve others.

Grant me these things, O God; through Jesus Christ my Lord. Amen.

USE IT OR LOSE IT

'After a long time the master of these servants returned and settled accounts with them. The man who had been given the twelve hundred and fifty pounds came up with another twelve hundred and fifty pounds. "Master," he said, "You handed over twelve hundred and fifty pounds to me. I have made a profit of another twelve hundred and fifty pounds." "Well done!" his master said to him. "You have shown yourself a good and trustworthy servant. Because you have shown that I could depend on you to do a small job well, I will give you a big job to do. Come and share your master's joy." The man who had been given the five hundred pounds came up. "Sir," he said, "you handed over five hundred pounds to me. I have made a profit of another five hundred pounds." "Well done!" his master said to him. "You have shown yourself to be a good and trustworthy servant. Because you have shown that I could depend on you to do a small job well, I will give you a big job to do. Come and share your master's joy."

'The man who had been given the two hundred and fifty pounds came up. "Sir," he said, "I am well aware that you are a shrewd and ruthless business man. I know that you have a habit of letting someone else do the work and of then taking the profits. I know you often step in and appropriate the results of some enterprise which you did not initiate. So I went and hid your two hundred and fifty pounds in a hole in the ground, because I was afraid to take the risk of doing anything with it. Here you are! Your money is safe!" "You lazy good-for-nothing!" his master answered. "You knew very well that I have a habit of letting other people do the work and of then taking the profits. You knew very well that I often step in and appropriate the results of some enterprise which I did not initiate. That is all the more reason why you ought to have lodged my money with the bankers, and then, when I came home, I would have got my money back with interest. Take the two hundred and fifty pounds from him, and give it to the man who has two thousand five hundred pounds. For, if any man has much, he will be given still more, but, if any man has nothing, he will lose even what he has. Fling the useless servant out into outer darkness. There will be tears and agony there."'

Matthew 25:14–30

I bind unto myself today
The power of God to hold and lead,
His eye to watch, his might to stay,
His ear to hearken to my need.
The wisdom of my God to teach,
His hand to guide, his shield to ward,
The word of God to give me speech,
His heavenly host to be my guard.

St Patrick's Breastplate Stanza 1

Saturday: Fifth Week

O God, give me wisdom,
> that I may always be able to know what is right to do,
> that I may be able to distinguish between that which
> is momentarily pleasant and that which is of
> lasting good.

Give me courage,
> always to do the right thing even when I am afraid to
> do it.

Give me self-control,
> so that no moment of impulse or passion may sweep
> me into mistakes I would regret.

Above all, give me love,
> that I may love all men as you love them, and that
> there should be no hatred in my heart, through
> Jesus Christ my Lord. Amen.

HELPING JESUS

'When the Son of Man comes in his glory, accompanied by all the angels, he will take his seat on his glorious throne. The people of every nation will be assembled before him, and he will separate them into two groups, in the same way as a shepherd separates the sheep from the goats. He will place the sheep on the right hand and the goats on the left. Then the king will say to those on the right: "You have earned my Father's blessing. Come and take possession of the kingdom, which has been prepared for you since the creation of the world. For, when I was hungry, you gave me food to eat; when I was thirsty, you gave me water to drink; when I was a stranger, you took me into your home circle; when I was naked, you clothed me; when I was ill, you came to visit me; when I was in prison, you came to see me." Then the good people will answer: "Sir, when did we see you hungry and feed you, or thirsty and give you water to drink? When did we see you a stranger and take you into our home circle, or naked and clothe you? When did we see you ill or in prison and come to visit you?" The king will answer: "The truth is that every time you did these things for one of my brothers, even for the least of them, you did them for me." Then he will say to those on the left: "God's curse is on you! Begone to the eternal fire which has been prepared for the devil and his angels! For, when I was hungry, you did not give me food to eat; when I was thirsty, you did not give me water to drink; when I was a stranger, you did not take me into your home circle; when I was naked, you did not clothe me; when I was ill and in prison, you did not come to visit me." At that, they will answer: "Sir, when did we see you hungry or thirsty or a stranger or naked or ill or in prison, and fail to give you help?" Then he will answer: "The truth is that every time you failed to do these things for one of these, even for the least of them, you failed to do them for me." These will go away to eternal punishment, but the good will go to eternal life.'

Matthew 25:31–46

Christ be with me, Christ within me,
Christ behind me, Christ before me,
Christ beside me, Christ to win me,
Christ to comfort and restore me.
Christ beneath me, Christ above me,
Christ in quiet, Christ in danger,
Christ in hearts of all that love me,
Christ in mouth of friend and stranger.
St Patrick's Breastplate Stanza 2

Sunday: Fifth Week

O God, help me to make this a day of rest, when I lay aside
my studies and my work so that I may go back to
them tomorrow refreshed.

Help me to make it a day of gladness, because I am glad
that on this day Jesus rose from the dead.

Help me to make it a day of learning, when I try to find
out something new about life and how to live it.

Help me to make it a day of friendship, when I spend some
time in my home and with my friends.

Help me to make it a day of worship, when I think about
you and remember your presence: through Jesus
Christ my Lord. Amen.

TREACHERY

It was then that the chief priests and the elders of the
people met in the palace of the High Priest, whose name
was Caiaphas, and discussed how to arrest Jesus by some
stratagem, and so to kill him. Their problem was that they
could not arrest him during the festival, because they
could not take the risk of a popular riot breaking out
among the people.

It was at this time that one of the Twelve, called Judas
Iscariot, went to the chief priests. 'What are you prepared
to give me,' he said, 'if I deliver him into your hands?'
They settled with him for five pounds. From then on Judas
was always looking for a good opportunity to deliver Jesus
into their hands.

Matthew 26:3–5, 14–16

Fill us, we pray thee, with thy light and life, that we may
show forth thy wondrous glory. Grant that thy love may
so fill our lives that we may count nothing too small to do
for thee, nothing too much to give, and nothing too hard

to bear. So teach us, Lord, to serve thee as thou deservest, to give and not to count the cost, to fight and not to heed the wounds, to toil and not to seek for rest, to labour and not to ask for any reward save that of knowing that we do thy will.

Ignatius Loyola

Monday: Sixth Week

O God, help me to go on at all times, when I would like to
stop.

Help me, when I feel discouraged because things
are so difficult, to keep on until I overcome the
difficulties.

Help me, when I get fed up because things are so
boring, to remember that I am laying the foundations on which my life will be built.

Help me, when I am driven almost to despair, and when
I lose hope of being and doing what I want to be and
do, to be ready to lose everything but hope.

Help me to remember that Jesus said that it is he who
endures to the end who will be saved, and help
me to keep going until I reach my goal; through
Jesus Christ my Lord. Amen.

LOVE'S EXTRAVAGANCE

When Jesus was in Bethany as the guest of Simon the leper,
a woman came up to him with an alabaster phial of very
expensive perfume, which she poured over his head as he
sat at table. The sight of her action annoyed the disciples.
'What is the point of this waste?' they said. 'This could have
been sold for a large sum of money, and the proceeds could
have been used to help the poor.' Jesus knew what they
were saying. 'Why are you distressing the woman?' he said.
'She has done a lovely thing to me. You have the poor with
you always, but you do not have me always. By pouring
this perfume over my body, she has by her action prepared
me for my burial. I tell you truly, wherever this Good News
is proclaimed all over the world, what she has done will be
told too, so that she will always be remembered.'

Matthew 26:6–13

O Lord our God, grant us grace to desire thee with our whole heart; that, so desiring, we may seek, and seeking find thee; and so finding thee may love thee; and loving thee, may hate those sins from which thou hast redeemed us.

St Anselm

Tuesday: Sixth Week

O God, give me the things which will make me a good
member of the community in which I live.

Give me the forgiving spirit, that I may forgive others,
as I hope that you will forgive me.

Give me the tolerant spirit that I may be quicker to
praise than to criticize, and that I may be more
eager to understand than to condemn.

Give me the unselfish spirit, that I may think even
more about the rights of others than about my
own rights.

Teach me what to remember and what to forget; to
forget all insults and injuries, and to remember
all that has been done for me by other people.

Help me always to aim at putting more into life than
I take out of it: through Jesus Christ my Lord.
Amen.

THE LAST SUPPER

When evening came, Jesus took his place at the table
with his twelve disciples. During the meal he said to
them: 'I tell you truly, one of you will betray me.' They
were very distressed, and each of them said to him:
'Master, surely it can't be me?' Jesus answered: 'It is one
who has dipped his bread with me in the dish who is
going to betray me. The Son of Man goes out on the road
the scripture says he must go. But tragic is the fate of the
man by whom the Son of Man is betrayed! It would have
been better for that man, if he had never been born!'
Judas, who was busy trying to betray him, said: 'Master,
surely it can't be me?' Jesus said to him: 'You have said it
yourself!'

During the meal Jesus took a loaf. He said the blessing over it, and broke it into pieces, and gave it to his disciples. 'Take! Eat!' he said. 'This means my body.' He took a cup, and gave thanks to God. He gave it to them and said: 'All of you drink it. This means my life-blood, through which the new relationship between man and God is made possible, the blood which is being shed for many, that their sins may be forgiven. I tell you, I shall not drink of this fruit of the vine, until the time comes when I drink it new with you in my Father's kingdom.'

Matthew 26:20–29

Thou, O Lord, who commandest us to ask, grant that we may receive. Thou hast put us upon seeking, let us be happy in finding; thou hast bidden us knock, we pray thee open to us. Be graciously pleased to direct and govern all our thoughts and actions, that for the future we may serve thee, and entirely devote ourselves to obeying thee. Accept us, we beseech thee, and draw us to thyself, that we may henceforth be thine by obedience and love, who are already all thine own as thy creatures – even thine, O Lord, who livest and reignest for ever and ever. Amen.

St Augustine

Wednesday: Sixth Week

O God, grant me in my life the basic virtues on which alone life can be built:

Courage, always to do what is right, no matter what the consequences;

Fidelity, always to be true to those who trust me;

Justice, that I may give all people their due;

Self-control, that I may be so completely in command of myself, that I may be fit always to serve others;

Charity, that I may live in love to all: through Jesus Christ my Lord. Amen.

GETHSEMANE

Then Jesus went with them to a place called Gethsemane. 'Sit here while I go over there and pray,' he said to his disciples. He took with him Peter and Zebedee's two sons, and he began to be distressed and distraught in mind. 'My soul is grief-stricken with a grief like death,' he said to them. 'Wait here and share my vigil.' He went a little farther, and flung himself face down on the ground in prayer. 'My Father,' he said, 'if it is possible, don't let this bitter ordeal come to me. But not what I will, but what you will.' He came to his disciples and found them sleeping. He said to Peter: 'So the three of you could not keep vigil with me for one hour? Sleeplessly watch and pray, for you may well all have to face your ordeal of temptation. I know that you mean well and that you want to do the right thing, but human nature is frail.' He went away a second time and prayed again. 'My Father,' he said, 'if there is no escape from this situation, unless I go through it to the bitter end, your will be done.' He came back again, and again he found them sleeping, for they could not keep their eyes open. Again he went away and left them, and again a third time he prayed the same prayer. Then he came to his disciples and said to them: 'Are you still lying there sleeping? The hour has come for the Son of Man to be delivered into the hands of sinful men. Up! On your way! The traitor is coming!'

Matthew 26:36–46

O Lord Jesu, our only health and our everlasting life, I give myself wholly unto thy will: being sure that the thing cannot perish which is committed unto thy mercy.

Thou, merciful Lord, wast born for my sake: thou didst suffer both hunger and thirst for my sake; thou didst preach and teach, didst pray and fast, for my sake: and finally thou gavest thy most precious body to die and thy blood to be shed on the cross, for my sake. Most merciful Saviour, let all these things profit me which thou freely hast given me. O Lord, into thy hands I commit my soul.

Primer of 1559

Thursday: Sixth Week

O God, I do not know what will happen to me today.
Whatever comes, help me to meet it well.

> If I have difficult things to do today, help me to keep
> on trying until they are done.
> If I will be tempted to do the wrong things, help me to
> resist temptation and to do the right.
> If things will go well with me, and I have good
> success, save me from all pride and keep me in
> humility.
> If I have to encounter failure, save me from despair,
> and help me to try again in hope.
> If I am hurt or injured in body or in spirit, keep me
> from anger and from the desire for revenge and
> give me the forgiving spirit.
> Give me your presence with me all through today,
> whatever light may shine or shadow fall:
> through Jesus Christ my Lord. Amen.

JESUS ON TRIAL

Those who had arrested Jesus took him to the house of
Caiaphas the High Priest, where the experts in the Law and
the elders had assembled. Peter followed him at a distance,
right into the courtyard of the High Priest's house. He went
in and sat down with the attendants to see the end.

The chief priests and the whole Sanhedrin made
repeated attempts to find fabricated evidence against
Jesus, which could be used to justify them in putting him
to death. Many witnesses who were prepared to perjure
themselves came forward, but the court was unable to
find any evidence upon which it could legitimately
proceed. At last two witnesses came forward and said:
'This man said: "I can demolish God's Temple, and in

three days I can rebuild it."' The High Priest stood up and said to Jesus: 'Have you no answer to these allegations which these witnesses are making against you?' Jesus remained silent. The High Priest said to him: 'I call on you to tell us on oath, in the name of the living God – are you the Messiah, the Son of God?' 'If you like to say so,' Jesus said. 'But I tell you, from now on you will see the Son of Man sitting at the right hand of Almighty God, and coming on the clouds of heaven.' At that the High Priest ripped his clothes in horror. 'This statement is blasphemy,' he said. 'What further witnesses do we need? You have actually here and now heard his blasphemous claim. What is your verdict?' They answered: 'He is guilty of a crime for which the penalty is death.' Then they spat in his face, and punched him with their clenched fists. Some of them slapped him across the face. 'Prophesy to us, Messiah,' they said. 'Who struck you?'

Matthew 26:57–68

Guide us, teach us, and strengthen us, O Lord, we beseech thee, until we become such as thou wouldst have us be: pure, gentle, truthful, high-minded, courteous, generous, able, dutiful and useful; for thy honour and glory. Amen.
Charles Kingsley

Friday: Sixth Week

O God, give me the gift of self-control.

> Give me control of my words that I may never say
> things of which afterwards I would be ashamed,
> or for which I would be sorry.
> Give me control of my temper, that I may never be
> swept away by anger.
> Give me control of my impulses and passions, that I
> may have everything under perfect control.

Lord Jesus, take me and control me so that all my deeds
and words and thoughts may be in captivity to your
obedience.
This I ask for your love's sake. Amen.

THE COLLAPSE OF LOYALTY

Peter was sitting outside in the courtyard. One of the
maidservants came up to him. 'You too were with Jesus
the Galilean,' she said. He denied it in front of them all.
'I have no idea what you're talking about,' he said. He
went out to the gateway. Another maidservant saw him.
She said to the people there: 'This man was with Jesus the
Nazarene.' Again he denied it. 'I swear I do not know the
man,' he said. Shortly afterwards the bystanders came
up to Peter and said to him: 'You certainly are one of
them. Indeed you are. Your Galilean accent makes it
obvious.' Peter swore he was telling the truth, and called
down curses on himself if he was not. 'I do not know
the man,' he said. Just then the cock crew, and Peter
remembered how Jesus had said: 'Before the cock crows,
you will disown me three times.' And he went out and
wept bitterly.

Matthew 26:69–75

Give us, O Lord, a mind after thine own heart, that we may delight to do thy will, O our God; and let thy Law be written on our hearts. Give us courage and resolution to do our duty, and a heart to be spent in thy service, and in doing all the good that possibly we can the few remaining days of our pilgrimage here on earth. Grant this, we humbly beseech thee for the sake of Jesus Christ thy son our Lord. Amen.

Archbishop John Tillotson

Saturday: Sixth Week

O God, I look back on this week now as it comes to an end.

> Forgive me for the things which I blush to remember. If I have hurt others; if I have failed my friends; if I have disappointed those who love me; Lord God, forgive.
>
> I thank you for all the good things which happened to me this week. For any kindness I have received; for any word of thanks or praise that I never expected; for any success that I have had; thank you, my Father.
>
> Bless everyone who has been kind to me and who has helped me this week; and bless anyone who injured me or hurt me, and make me able to forgive.
>
> Help me to learn the lesson life is meant to teach me, and not to make the same mistakes over and over again, and so help me to be better in the days that lie ahead; through Jesus Christ my Lord. Amen.

THE CROSS

From twelve o'clock midday until three o'clock in the afternoon there was darkness over the whole land. About three o'clock in the afternoon Jesus gave a great shout: 'Eli, Eli, lama sabachthani?' which means: 'My God, my God, why have you abandoned me?' When some of the bystanders heard this, they said: 'He is calling Elijah!' One of them at once ran and took a sponge and soaked it in vinegar and put it on a cane, and offered it to him to drink. The others said: 'Wait! Let us see if Elijah is coming to save him.' Jesus again shouted at the top of his voice, and died.

The curtain of the Temple which veiled the Holy of Holies was ripped from top to bottom, and the ground was shaken and the rocks were split. The tombs were burst open, and the bodies of many of the people of God who slept in death were raised to life. They came out of their tombs, and after his resurrection they went into the holy city, and appeared to many. When the company commander and his men who were watching Jesus saw the earthquake and the things which were happening, they were awe-stricken. 'Beyond a doubt,' they said, 'this man was indeed a son of God.'

Matthew 27:45–54

O Lord Jesus Christ, give us grace, we beseech thee, this day to do all we have to do in thy name. May we live as those who bear thy holy name, and solely to the glory of thy name. May we refer all things solely to thee, and receive all from thee. Be thou the beginning and the end of all, the pattern whom we are to copy, the redeemer in whom is our strength, the master whom we are to serve, the friend to whom we may look for comfort and sympathy. May we fix our eyes on thee as our help, our aim, the centre of our being, our everlasting friend. O thou who hast so looked on us that we may see thee, set thine eyes upon us, we beseech thee; steady our unsteadfastness, unite us to thyself, and guide us in whatever path thou seest fit to lead us, till of thine infinite mercy thou wilt bring us to thine eternal presence; for thine own name's sake we ask it. Amen.

Canon Edward Pusey

Sunday: Sixth Week

Help me, O God, to use this, your day, to improve myself
in every way.

Help me to take the physical exercise which will
improve my physical fitness.

Help me to read some good book or to listen to some
wise teacher to improve my mental fitness.

Help me to think about Jesus, and in my mind's eye
to see him going about doing good, so that his
love for all men may increase within my heart.

And help me today to do something for someone who
needs my help, so that the love within my heart
may turn to deeds; through Jesus Christ my Lord.
Amen.

THE RISEN CHRIST

Late on the Sabbath, just as the day was breaking on the
Sunday, Mary from Magdala and the other Mary came to
look at the tomb. There was a great earthquake, for the
angel of the Lord came down from heaven, and came
and rolled away the stone, and sat on it. His face shone
like lightning, and his clothes were as white as snow. The
guards were shaken with fear, and lay like dead men.
The angel said to the women: 'Do not be afraid. I know
that you are looking for Jesus who was crucified. He is not
here, for he has risen, as he said he would. Come! See for
yourselves the place where his body lay. Hurry and tell his
disciples that he has risen from the dead, and that he is
going on ahead of you into Galilee. You will meet him
there. That is the message I have for you.' They hurried
away from the tomb in mingled awe and great joy, and
ran to tell the news to the disciples. Suddenly Jesus was
standing in their path. 'Joy be with you,' he said. They

went up to him, and clasped his feet, and knelt before him.
Then Jesus said to them: 'Don't be afraid. Go and tell my
brothers to leave for Galilee. They will see me there.'

Matthew 28:1–10

Give us, O Lord, purity of lips, clean and innocent hearts,
and rectitude of action; give us humility, patience, self-
wisdom and understanding, the spirit of counsel and
strength, the spirit of knowledge and godliness, and of thy
fear; make us ever to seek thy face with all our heart, all
our soul, all our mind; grant us to have a contrite and
humbled heart in thy presence, to prefer nothing to thy
love. Have mercy upon us, we humbly beseech thee;
through Jesus our Lord. Amen.

Gallican Sacramentary

Prayers for Special Occasions

Christmas

O God, on this Christmas Day, I thank you for Jesus.

> I thank you that he took our ordinary life upon himself.
> I thank you that he was born not in a palace but in a stable.
> I thank you that it was not earthly wealth and ease that he knew, but that he was born into a humble home, where he had to work for a living.
> I thank you that he had to grow up and to learn as any child must, and that he was obedient to his parents as anyone must be.
> Help me to be like him, and grant that on this Christmas Day I may think more of giving than of getting.
> I thank you for a happy home. Grant that I may show my gratitude for all your gifts by living more like him who was born in Bethlehem on the first Christmas Day.
> This I ask for your love's sake. Amen.

THE WORD BECAME FLESH

When the world began, the Word was already there. The Word was with God, and the nature of the Word was the same as the nature of God. The Word was there in the beginning with God. It was through the agency of the Word that everything else came into being. Without the Word not one single thing came into being. As for the whole creation, the Word was the life principle in it, and that life was the light of men. The light continues to shine in the darkness, and the darkness has never extinguished it.

On to the stage of history there came a man sent from God. His name was John. The purpose of his coming was to declare the truth, and the truth he declared was about the light. The aim of his declaration was to persuade all men to believe. He himself was not the light. His only function was to tell men about the light. The real light, the light which enlightens every man, was just about to come into the world. He was in the world, and, although it was through him that the world came into being, the world failed to recognize him. It was to his own home that he came, but his own people refused to receive him. But to all who did receive him he gave the privilege of becoming God's children. That privilege was given to those who do believe that he really is what he is. They were born, not by the common processes of physical birth, not as the consequence of some moment of sexual passion, not as a result of any man's desire. Their birth came from God.

John 1:1–13

Moonless darkness stands between,
Past, O Past, no more be seen!
But the Bethlehem star may lead me
To the sight of him who freed me
From the self that I have been.
Make me pure, Lord: thou art holy;
Make me meek, Lord: thou wert lowly;
Now beginning, and alway:
Now begin, on Christmas day.
Gerard Manley Hopkins

New Year's Day

O God, you can make all things new.

> I thank you for this New Year, and for the chance to begin again.
> Help me this year to be kinder and more considerate than I have been up to now.
> Help me to work and study harder than ever I did before.
> Help me to conquer the temptations which will attack me.
> Help me all through this year to aim high and to reach my target; through Jesus Christ my Lord. Amen.

FROM EVERLASTING TO EVERLASTING

Lord, thou hast been our dwelling place in all generations.
Before the mountains were brought forth,
> or ever thou hadst formed the earth and the world,
> from everlasting to everlasting thou art God.

Thou turnest man back to the dust, and sayest, 'Turn back, O children of men!'
For a thousand years in thy sight are but as yesterday when it is past, or as a watch in the night.

Let thy work be manifest to thy servants,
> and thy glorious power to their children.
Let the favour of the Lord our God be upon us,
> and establish thou the work of our hands upon us,
> yea, the work of our hands establish thou it.
>> *Psalm 90:1–4, 16–17*

Eternal God, who makest all things new, and abidest for ever the same: Grant us to begin this year in thy faith, and to continue it in thy favour; that, guided in all our doings, and guarded all our days, we may spend our lives in thy service, and finally, by thy grace, attain the glory of everlasting life; through Jesus Christ our Lord.

Order of Divine Service for Public Worship

Good Friday

Lord Jesus, help me to remember that on this day you were
crucified for us.

And grant that as I remember your love and your
suffering I may be lost in wonder, love and praise,
and that I may come to love you as you first loved
me.
For your love's sake I ask it. Amen.

THE CROSS

One of the criminals who had been crucified kept hurling
insults at Jesus. 'Are you not the Messiah?' he said. 'Save
yourself and us!' The other sternly reprimanded him.
'Have you no reverence for God?' he said. 'You have been
sentenced to the same punishment as he has been, and we
with justice, for we are getting what we deserve for our
misdeeds, but he has committed no crime. Jesus,' he said,
'remember me when you come into your Kingdom.' Jesus
said to him: 'Very certainly you will be with me in
Paradise today.'

By this time it was about twelve o'clock midday, and
darkness came over the whole land until three o'clock in
the afternoon, for the sun was in eclipse. The curtain of the
Temple which veiled the Holy of Holies was ripped down
the middle. Jesus shouted at the top of his voice. Then he
said: 'Father, into your hands I entrust my spirit.' When
he had said this, he died.

Luke 23:39–46

O blessed Saviour, draw us; draw us by the cords of thy love; draw us by the sense of thy goodness; draw us by thyself; draw us by the unspotted purity and beauty of thy example; draw us by the merit of thy precious death and by the power of thy Holy Spirit; draw us, good Lord, and we shall run after thee. Amen.

The Rev Dr Isaac Barrow

Easter Day

Lord Jesus, I thank you that on the first Easter Day you
conquered death and the grave and rose to life again.
I thank you that you are not only a memory, but that you
are also a living presence.
I thank you that you promised to be with us to the end of
the world and beyond.
Help me to remember that all life is lived in your unseen
presence, and help me to make it fit for you to see.
This I ask for your love's sake. Amen.

THE GREAT RECOGNITION

On Sunday Mary from Magdala went to the tomb so early
in the morning that it was still dark. When she saw that
the stone had been removed from the tomb, she went running to Simon Peter and to the other disciple, the disciple
who was specially dear to Jesus. 'They have taken away
the Master from the tomb,' she said, 'and we don't know
where they have put him.' Peter and the other disciple set
out on the way to the tomb. They both began to run. The
other disciple ran on ahead, faster than Peter, and
reached the tomb first. He stooped down and looked in,
and saw the linen grave-clothes lying there, but he did not
go in. Simon Peter arrived after him, and went into the
tomb. He saw the linen grave-clothes lying there, and he
saw the towel, which had been round Jesus' head, lying
not with the other grave-clothes, but still in its folds,
separately in a place all by itself. Then the other disciple,
who had arrived at the tomb first, went in, and when he
saw the inside of the tomb he was convinced. As yet they
did not understand that scripture said that Jesus had to
rise from the dead. So the disciples went back home.

John 20:1–10

O merciful God, the Father of our Lord Jesus Christ, who is the resurrection and the life; in whom whosoever believeth shall live, though he die; and whosoever liveth and believeth in him shall not die eternally. We bless thy holy name for all thy servants departed in this life in thy faith and fear; beseeching thee to give us grace so to follow their good example that with them we may be partakers of thy heavenly kingdom. Grant this, O Father, for Jesus Christ's sake, our only advocate and redeemer. Amen.

Sarum Missal

Whit Sunday

God, grant to me also the help of your Holy Spirit.

Let your Holy Spirit guide my thinking so that all my
    thoughts may be clean, and so that I may reach a
    solution to all the problems which perplex me.
Let your Holy Spirit guide my footsteps, so that I may
    never lose the way or take the wrong way.
Let your Holy Spirit control my tongue so that I may never
    speak a word which is untrue, unclean or unkind.
Let your Holy Spirit guide and direct my whole life so that
    I may keep to the straight pathway until my journey's
    end; through Jesus Christ my Lord. Amen.

THE COMING OF THE SPIRIT

The disciples were all passing the day of Pentecost together. All of a sudden a sound came from the sky like a blast
of violent wind, and it filled the whole house where they
were sitting. There appeared to them what looked like
tongues of fire, which divided themselves up, and settled
on each one of them. They were all filled with the Holy
Spirit, and began to speak in other languages, as the
Spirit enabled them to speak.

There were Jews staying in Jerusalem, devout men
who had come from every nation under the sun. When
they heard the sound of this, they came in their crowds.
They were bewildered, because each of them was hearing
the disciples speaking in his own language. They were
astonished and amazed. 'Aren't all these men who are
speaking Galileans?' they said. 'How then is it that
each one of us hears them speaking in the language we
have spoken since we were born? Parthians and Medes
and Elamites, those whose homes are in Mesopotamia,
Judaea and Cappadocia, Pontus and Asia, Phrygia and

Pamphylia, Egypt and the Cyrenian parts of Libya, visitors from Rome, Jews and converts to Judaism, Cretans and Arabians, we are hearing them telling of God's great deeds in our own languages.' They were all astonished, and completely at a loss what to make of it. 'What is the meaning of this?' they said to each other. Others treated the whole affair as a jest. 'They are full of new wine,' they said.

Acts 2:1–13

God, who as at this time didst teach the hearts of thy faithful people by sending to them the light of thy Holy Spirit, grant us by the same Spirit to have a right judgement in all things and evermore to rejoice in his holy comfort; through the merits of Christ Jesus our saviour, who liveth and reigneth with thee in the unity of the same Spirit, one God, world without end. Amen.

Gregorian Sacramentary

First Day of Term

O God, today is for me the first day of a new term.

I thank you for everyone who has taught me and for all
that I have learned up to now.
Help me to use this new term wisely and to use it well.
Help me to use to the full the opportunities of learning
which will come to me.
Help me to count as a day wasted when I do not learn
something new.

All through this term help me to be friendly towards my
fellow pupils and respectful towards my teachers.
Help me to work hard and to play hard, so that I may be
a good citizen of my school; through Jesus Christ my
Lord. Amen.

THE EXCELLENT THINGS

Never lose your Christian joy. Let me say it again! Never
lose it! You must make it common knowledge that you
never insist on the letter of the law. It will not be long now
until the Lord comes. Don't worry about anything. In
every circumstance of life tell God about the things you
want to ask him for in your prayers and your requests to
him, and bring him your thanks too. And God's peace,
which is beyond both our understanding and our contriv-
ing, will stand guard over your hearts and minds, because
your life is linked for ever with the life of Christ Jesus.

It only remains to say, brothers, that your thoughts
must continually dwell on everything that is true, on
everything that is nobly serious, on everything that is
right, on everything that is pure, on everything that is
lovely, on everything that is honourable, on all that men
call excellence, and on all that wins men's praise. You

must keep putting into practice the lessons you have learned from me, the instructions you have received from me, and the example I have given you in speech and in action. And then the God of peace will be with you.

Philippians 4:4–9

O God of time and eternity, who makest us creatures of time, to the end that when time is over we may attain to thy blessed eternity. With time, which is thy gift, give us also wisdom to redeem the time lest our day of grace be lost, for the sake of Christ Jesus our Lord. Amen.

Christina G. Rossetti

Examination Time

O God, give me your help at this examination time.
Keep me from being nervous and keep me calm, so that I
    will be able to do my best.
If I am not prepared, I have no excuse. If I am prepared,
    and if I have done my best, give me the calm and the
    freedom from nerves I need to do well; through Jesus
    Christ my Lord. Amen.

THE YOKE IN YOUTH

The steadfast love of the Lord never ceases,
    his mercies never come to an end;
they are new every morning;
    great is thy faithfulness.
'The Lord is my portion,' says my soul,
    'therefore I will hope in him.'

The Lord is good to those who wait for him,
    to the soul that seeks him.
It is good that one should wait quietly
    for the salvation of the Lord.
It is good for a man that he bear the
    yoke in his youth.
Lamentations 3:22–27

O God, the sovereign good of the soul, who requirest the
hearts of all thy children, deliver us from all sloth in thy
work, all coldness in thy cause; and grant us by looking
unto thee to rekindle our love, and by waiting upon thee
to renew our strength; through Jesus Christ our Lord.
Amen.

William Bright

The Day of the Match

O God, I thank you that you have made me strong enough
   in limb and fit enough in body to play in this match
   today.
Help me to play hard but to play fair. Make me such that
   I would rather lose the match than win by unfair or
   foul means.
If we win keep me from boasting about it, and if we lose
   keep me from making excuses; through Jesus Christ
   my Lord. Amen.

PRESSING TO THE GOAL

Beware of these dogs! Beware of these manufacturers of
wickedness! Beware of those whose circumcision is no
better than mutilation! It is we who are really circumcised,
for we offer God a worship directed by his Spirit. Our pride
is in Christ Jesus. We place no reliance on human ex-
ternals, although I might well base my claims on such
things. If anyone thinks that he can rely on physical
marks and human achievements, I have an even stronger
claim. I was circumcised on the eighth day after I was
born. I am a pure-blooded Israelite. I belong to the tribe of
Benjamin. I am a Hebrew and the son of Hebrew parents.
In my attitude to the Jewish law I was a Pharisee. So
enthusiastic was my devotion to the law that I was a
persecutor of the church. As far as the goodness which the
law prescribes and demands is concerned, I was beyond
criticism. But whatever achievements in my life and
career I would once have reckoned among the profits of
life, I have written off as a dead loss for the sake of Christ.
Yes, and more than that – I am prepared to write off everything as a dead loss for the sake of getting to know Christ
Jesus my Lord, for that knowledge is something which
surpasses everything in the world. For his sake I have

abandoned everything, and I regard all else as of no more value than filth for the garbage heap. For me the only thing of value in the world is to gain Christ, and to make my life one with his. I am not right with God through any legalistic achievement of my own. All I want is the relationship with God which only God himself can give me, all founded on faith in Christ. My one aim is to know Christ, and to experience the power of his resurrection, and to share with him in his sufferings. My aim is to die the death he died, so that, if it may be, I may reach the resurrection from the dead.

I do not claim that I have already attained this, or that I have already reached perfection. I press on to try to grasp that for which Christ Jesus has already grasped me. Brothers, I do not regard myself as having already grasped the prize. But I have one aim in life – to forget what lies behind, and to strain every nerve to reach what lies ahead. And so I press on to the goal to win the prize to which God in Christ Jesus calls me upward and onward.

Philippians 3:2–14

Grant that we may walk as Christ walked; Grant that what the Spirit was in him, such he may be also in us; Grant that our lives may be refashioned after the pattern of his life; Grant that we may do today here on earth what Christ would have done, and in the way he would have done it; Grant that we may become vessels of his grace, instruments of his will – to thy honour and glory; through Jesus Christ our Lord. Amen.

J. H. Jowett

End of Term

O God, thank you for bringing me to the end of another
   term.
Forgive me for the time I have wasted, and for the opportunities I have missed.
Thank you for all that I have learned during this term,
   and thank you for any new friends I have made and
   all the old friends I have kept.
Thank you for those who encouraged me when I was
   feeling discouraged, and thank you for those who
   had patience with me when I was very annoying.
Help me to remember all that I have been taught, so that
   when I come back next term I may make even better
   progress; through Jesus Christ my Lord. Amen.

THE ARMOUR OF THE SPIRIT

Finally, your union with the Lord and with his mighty
power must give you a dynamic strength. Put on the
complete armour which God can give you, and then you
will be able to resist the stratagems of the Devil. For our
struggle is not against any human foe; it is against
demonic rulers and authorities, against the cosmic
powers of this dark world, against spiritual forces of evil
in the heavens. So then, take the complete armour which
God can give you, and then, when the evil day comes, you
will be able to see things through to the end, and to
remain erect. So then take your stand. Buckle the belt of
truth round your waist. Put on righteousness for a breastplate. Put preparedness to preach the gospel of peace on
your feet like shoes. Through thick and thin take faith as
your shield. With it you will be able to extinguish all the
flaming arrows of the Evil One. Take salvation as your
helmet. Take the sword the Spirit gives. That sword is the
word of God. Keep on praying fervently, and asking God

for what you need, and on every occasion let the Spirit be the atmosphere in which you pray. To that end sleeplessly and always persevere in your requests to God for all God's consecrated people. Pray for me too, and ask God to give me a message when I have to speak. Pray that I may be able fearlessly to tell men the secret of the good news, for which I am an ambassador, though now in chains. I need your prayers to enable me to speak it with the fearlessness with which I ought to speak.

Ephesians 6:10–20

Grant, O Lord, that what we have said with our lips, we may believe in our hearts and practise in our lives; and of thy mercy keep us faithful unto the end; for Christ's sake. Amen.

John Hunter

Going to Work for the First Time

O God, bless me as I go out to work for the first time.

In my work help me always to do my best, so that I may
be a workman who never has any need to be
ashamed.

Help me to work equally hard whether I am watched or
not, always remembering that you see me, and
always trying to make my work good enough to offer
to you.

Help me always to remember that Jesus worked in the
carpenter's shop in Nazareth, and help me to be as
good a workman as he was.

This I ask for your love's sake. Amen.

A GOOD WORKMAN

Remember Jesus Christ, risen from the dead, descended
from David. This is what my gospel teaches. It is for the
sake of that gospel that I am at present suffering, even to
the length of being imprisoned as a criminal. But no one
can put the word of God in prison. It is for the sake of God's
chosen ones that I can pass the breaking-point and not
break. I want them too to win that salvation which is ours
because of what Christ Jesus has done for us, and with it
the glory that is eternal. It has been said, and said truly:

If we have died with him,
　　we shall live with him;
if we endure,
　　we shall reign with him;
if we deny him,
　　he too will deny us;
if we are faithless,
　　he remains faithful,
　　for he cannot deny himself.

Keep on reminding them of all this. Charge them before God not to engage in pugnacious debates about verbal niceties. Debates like that are an unprofitable occupation, and do nothing but undermine the faith of the hearers. Do your best to present yourself to God as a man of sterling worth, a workman who has no need to be ashamed of his work, a sound expositor of the true word.

2 Timothy 2:8–15

Do thou thyself, O Lord, send out thy light and thy truth, and enlighten the eyes of our minds to understand thy divine Word. Give us grace to be hearers of it, and not hearers only, but doers of the Word, that we may bring forth good fruit abundantly and be counted worthy of the kingdom of heaven. And to thee, O Lord our God, we ascribe glory and thanksgiving, now and for ever. Amen.

Liturgy of the Greek Church

For Friends

I thank you for my friends, for those who understand me
better than I understand myself, for those who know
me at my worst and still like me, for those who have
forgiven me when I had no right to expect to be
forgiven.

Help me to be as true to my friends as I would wish them
to be to me.

Help me to take the first step to get into touch again with
friends from whom I have drifted apart.

And help me to have no bitterness but only forgiveness to
any of my friends who failed or who turned against
me; through Jesus Christ my Lord. Amen.

TRUE FRIENDSHIP

Then they lifted up their voices and wept again; and
Orpah kissed her mother-in-law, but Ruth clung to her.

And she said, 'See, your sister-in-law has gone back to
her people and to her gods; return after your sister-in-law.'
But Ruth said, 'Entreat me not to leave you or to return
from following you; for where you go I will go, and where
you lodge I will lodge; your people shall be my people, and
your God my God; where you die I will die, and there will
I be buried. May the Lord do so to me and more also if even
death parts me from you.' And when Naomi saw that she
was determined to go with her, she said no more.

Ruth 1:14–18

May thy Spirit hallow, and thy Grace fortify, O blessed Lord, friends and others for whom we would seek thine aid: those of closest tie, those of greatest need.

May thy divine power protect and provide for them. May thy peace comfort them. May thy pardon reassure them, and thy precious blood redeem them. May thy prosperity attend them. May daily progress be theirs in the heavenly way; through Christ Jesus our Lord. Amen.

A Chain of Prayer Across the Ages

In the Time of Illness

O God, bless me in this illness that has come to me.

Make me a good patient, always obedient to the doctor's
    instructions, always cheerful and always uncom-
    plaining.

I remember before you all other people who are ill and in
    pain. Help them and help me to get better soon.

Thank you for all the people who look after me so well,
    and for all that they do for me.

Help me to show my gratitude by never grumbling or
    complaining, and by being cheerful even when being
    cheerful is difficult; through Jesus Christ my Lord.
    Amen.

GOD'S DELIVERANCE

I love the Lord, because he has heard
    my voice and my supplications.
Because he inclined his ear to me,
    therefore I will call on him as long as I live.
The snares of death encompassed me;
    the pangs of Sheol laid hold on me;
    I suffered distress and anguish.
Then I called on the name of the Lord:
    'O Lord, I beseech thee, save my life!'

Gracious is the Lord, and righteous;
    our God is merciful.
The Lord preserves the simple;
    when I was brought low, he saved me.
Return, O my soul, to your rest;
    for the Lord has dealt bountifully with you.

For thou hast delivered my soul from death,
    my eyes from tears,
    my feet from stumbling.

Psalm 116:1–8

O Lord, forasmuch as it is an easy thing with thee to give life to the dead, restore, we pray thee, to the sick their former health, and grant that they who seek the healing of thy heavenly mercy, may also obtain the remedies necessary for the body; through Jesus Christ our Lord. Amen.

Gothic Missal

In Disappointment

O God, you know me better than I know myself, and you
know how disappointed I have been at this time.

The thing that I had set my heart on was not for me.
The friends I trusted proved untrue.
I honestly tried so hard, and I failed.

Help me, O God, to accept things as they are. Help me
not to waste my time on vain regrets and unhappy
memories. Help me to begin again and to try again.
Help me always to look forward and not back. Help
me to forget the things that are behind and ever to
press forward to the things which are ahead; through
Jesus Christ my Lord. Amen.

WHY ARE YOU CAST DOWN?

Oh send out thy light and thy truth;
    let them lead me,
let them bring me to thy holy hill
    and to thy dwelling!
Then I will go to the altar of God,
    to God my exceeding joy;
and I will praise thee with the lyre,
    O God, my God.

Why are you cast down, O my soul,
    and why are you disquieted within me?
Hope in God; for I shall again praise him,
    my help and my God.

Psalm 43:3–5

Stretch forth, O Lord, thy mercy over all thy servants everywhere, even the right hand of heavenly help, that they may seek thee with their whole heart, and obtain what they rightly ask for; through Jesus Christ our Lord. Amen.

Gelasian Sacramentary

In Success

O God, I thank you that I have done well. I thank you for
    success.

Keep me from being conceited; keep me humble.
Help me to remember all those to whom I owe my success,
    those who taught me and trained me, and who
    encouraged me when I was tired and depressed.
Help me not to sit back and admire myself, but help me
    to see that, whatever I have achieved there are still
    higher heights to climb, and still further goals to
    reach. Whatever praise I receive, help me always to
    be my own severest critic; through Jesus Christ my
    Lord. Amen.

TRUE GOODNESS

If there is such a thing as Christian encouragement, if
there is such a thing as love's comforting power, if you and
I are really sharing in the partnership which only the Holy
Spirit can make possible, if you really wish to show me a
heartfelt sympathy which is like the mercy of God, make
my joy complete by being in perfect harmony of mind, by
joining in a common love for God and for each other, by
sharing in a common life, by taking every decision in
unity of mind, by never acting from motives of competi-
tive rivalry or in the conceited desire for empty prestige. If
you want to make my joy complete, instead of that each
of you must humbly think the other better than himself;
each of you must concentrate, not on his own interest, but
on the interests of others also. Try always to have the same
attitude to life as Jesus had.

He shared the very being of God,
but he did not regard his equality to God
   as a thing to be clutched to himself.
So far from that, he emptied himself,
      and really and truly became a servant,
and was made for a time exactly like men.
In a human form that all could see,
      he accepted such a depth of humiliation
      that he was prepared to die,
      and to die on a cross.
That is why God has given him the highest place,
      and has conferred on him
      the name that is greater than any name,
so that at the name of Jesus every creature
      in heaven, and on earth, and beneath the earth
should kneel in reverence and submission,
and so that everything which has a voice
      should openly declare
      that Jesus Christ is Lord,
and thus bring glory to God the Father.

Philippians 2:1–11

O Lord, give us more charity, more self-denial, more likeness to thee. Teach us to sacrifice our comforts to others,
and our likings for the sake of doing good. Teach us that
it is better to give than to receive, better to forget ourselves
than to put ourselves forward; better to minister than to
be ministered unto. And unto thee, the God of love, be all
glory and praise, both now and for ever more. Amen.

Henry Alford

For a Birthday

O God, today another year of life is finished and another
     year of life has begun.
Thank you for bringing me safely through another year.
Grant that I may not only be a year older, but also a year
     wiser.
Help me to profit by experience, so that I may not make
     the same mistakes over and over again.
O God, at the end of one year of life and at the beginning
     of another, I cannot help remembering all that I
     meant to do and to be in the year that is just past, and
     how little I have actually done. Help me in this incom-
     ing year really to carry out my resolutions and inten-
     tions, so that when I come to the end of it there may
     be no regrets; through Jesus Christ my Lord. Amen.

THE PASSING YEARS

Lord, thou hast been our dwelling place
     in all generations.
Before the mountains were brought forth,
     or ever thou hadst formed the earth and the world,
     from everlasting to everlasting thou art God.

Thou turnest man back to the dust,
     and sayest, 'Turn back, O children of men!'
For a thousand years in thy sight
     are but as yesterday when it is past,
     or as a watch in the night.

Thou dost sweep men away; they are like a dream,
     like grass which is renewed in the morning:
in the morning it flourishes and is renewed;
     in the evening it fades and withers.

For we are consumed by thy anger;
　　by thy wrath we are overwhelmed.
Thou hast set our iniquities before thee,
　　our secret sins in the light of thy countenance.

For all our days pass away under thy wrath,
　　our years come to an end like a sigh.
The years of our life are threescore and ten,
　　or even by reason of strength fourscore;
yet their span is but toil and trouble;
　　they are soon gone, and we fly away.

Who considers the power of thy anger,
　　and thy wrath according to the fear of thee?
So teach us to number our days
　　that we may get a heart of wisdom.

Psalm 90:1–12

It is my birthday, Lord Jesus, my saviour, and I thank thee
for giving me the wonderful gift of life. I pray thee that I
may use my life rightly, that I may try to grow braver,
kinder, wiser and truer year by year. I thank thee for all
the joys of the past year, and pray thee to bless me through
the coming one. Help me to conquer my faults and live
more to thy glory. Grant me thy grace to help all those
around me, and to try and make them happy. Be with me
step by step all through this new year, and keep me safe
unto the end; for thy sake. Amen.

A Chain of Prayer Across the Ages

At the End of the Year

O God, as this year comes to an end, I think back and
    remember.
I remember the time I have wasted.
I remember the things I meant to do and have not done.
I remember the resolutions I made and broke.
I remember the laziness which resented any effort.
I remember how easily side-tracked I have been.
I have so often been lured away from the things that
    matter by the things which do not matter.
Forgive me for the past and strengthen me for the future, and
    help me so to live this year that at the end of it I may
    have no regrets; through Jesus Christ my Lord. Amen.

THE LAW OF SUCCESS

Blessed is the man
    who walks not in the counsel of the wicked,
    nor stands in the way of sinners,
        nor sits in the seat of scoffers;
    but his delight is in the law of the Lord,
        and on his law he meditates day and night.
He is like a tree
    planted by streams of water,
that yields its fruit in its season,
    and its leaf does not wither.
In all that he does he prospers.

The wicked are not so,
    but are like chaff which the wind drives away.
Therefore the wicked will not stand in the judgement,
    nor sinners in the congregation of the righteous;
for the Lord knows the way of the righteous,
    but the way of the wicked will perish.

Psalm 1

O Lord, in whose hands are life and death, by whose power I am sustained, and by whose mercy I am spared, look down upon me with pity. Forgive me that I have until now so much neglected the duty which thou hast assigned to me, and suffered the days and hours of which I must give account to pass away without any endeavour to accomplish thy will. Make me to remember, O God, that every day is thy gift and ought to be used according to thy command. Grant me, therefore, so to repent of my negligence, that I may obtain mercy from thee, and pass the time which thou shalt yet allow me in diligent performance of thy commands, through Jesus Christ. Amen.

Samuel Johnson

A Little Prayer Diary

CHRISTOPHER HERBERT

Prayer, like talking to friends, can be easy. You don't have to learn any new skills or techniques; you don't have to learn a new language; you don't have to pass any tests: all you have to do is talk.

A Little Prayer Diary shows you how to make the most of your prayer time. A 31-day diary of 'conversation starters', it combines daily meditations with prayers which different people across the ages have found helpful. It is a delightful mixture of old and new.

With simple guidance on ways of praying and using the Bible in prayer, this is a charming and highly practical introduction to prayer.

Christopher Herbert has recently been appointed as the Bishop of St Albans. He began his career as a teacher and youth worker in Hereford, and later became Director of Religious Education in the Diocese. In 1981 he was appointed Anglican Vicar of the Bourne in Farnham, and subsequently became Archdeacon of Dorking. He is somewhat of an authority on prayer, with bestselling books to his credit such as Praying With Children *and* The Prayer Garden. *He is married with two children.*

Praying The Gospel

A focus on Jesus Christ, the Way, the Truth, the Life

DAVID KONSTANT

The first steps towards prayer are often the hardest. We stumble to find the right words even though we sometimes feel the urge to pray. Here, David Konstant guides us through words which are the beginning of prayer – words of scripture and of the great spiritual writers which help make sense of everyday life – words which bring us into the presence of Christ, the Way, the Truth, the Life.

With further suggestions for morning and evening meditation, this book offers, in Bishop Konstant's words, 'a small scaffolding for prayer'.

David Konstant was born in London in 1930 and ordained a Catholic priest in 1954. Auxiliary Bishop in Westminster and later Bishop of Leeds, he was appointed Chairman of the English and Welsh Bishops' Department for Education.

Peace of Heart in All Things

Meditations for each day of the year

BROTHER ROGER OF TAIZÉ

In 1940 a young Swiss man settled in the tiny village of Taizé, situated amid the Burgundy vineyards between the ancient monastic foundations of Cluny and Citeaux. Roger Schutz offered shelter and hiding to political refugees, particularly Jews. At the same time he gathered around him a few men of different Christian denominations, the pioneers of the great ecumenical community-to-be.

Peace of Heart in All Things is a brand new book from Brother Roger. It distils the Christian teaching offered throughout more than 50 years spent in community, teaching which emphasizes how Christ can bring us together rather than divide us.

This book has been written for anybody to whom the mission of Taizé appeals and particularly the young people who visit in such numbers during the summer months. It is a book to be kept, treasured and consulted at regular intervals.

Since Brother Roger founded the community in the Second World War, the community of Taizé has grown to 80 brothers from all over the world. It hosts meetings for many thousands of young people every summer and a major meeting in a European city every year.

Dare to Dream

*A prayer and worship anthology from around
the world*

COMPILED AND EDITED BY GEOFFREY DUNCAN

In a world filled with poverty, oppression and discrimination, our dreams for a better future can, at times, seem impossible to fulfil. Our responsibilities towards one another as God's people can seem burdensome and overpowering.

This anthology, compiled by the Council for World Mission, aims to motivate all of us to explore contemporary issues that will be present for years to come, and be challenged to action.

Its colourful prayers, litanies, poetry and readings, drawn from a rich variety of Christian experiences from around the world, combine to draw us into a deeper understanding of world issues, and thus provide an excellent foundation for worship and prayer, both personal and public.

Dare to Dream will enable you to do just that; to keep your dreams of a better world alive.

Daily Readings with Mother Teresa

EDITED BY TERESA DE BERTODANO

'Yesterday is always today with God. Therefore today in the world Jesus stands covered with our sins in the distressing disguise of my Sister, my Brother. Do I want Him? … Jesus comes as bread of life to be eaten – to be consumed by us. This is how He loves us. Jesus comes in our human life as the hungry one, the other, hoping to be fed with the bread of our lives, our hearts, our hands. In loving and serving we prove that we have been created in the image and likeness of God: for God is love and when we love we are like God. This is what Jesus meant when He said, "Be you perfect as your heavenly father is perfect."'

Mother Teresa has dedicated her life to the care of the sick and dying in Calcutta and beyond.

In this beautiful collection of readings by Mother Teresa and others, we see her total commitment to imitate Christ in his love of the poor, and to learn how to pray.

Daily Readings with Mother Teresa offers a perfect introduction for all those wanting to discover more about this extraordinary woman and her work.

Daily Readings with William Barclay

EDITED BY RONALD BARCLAY

'Eternal God, who givest us the day for work and the night for rest, grant unto us, as we go to rest, a good night's sleep; and wake us refreshed on the morrow, better able to serve thee and to serve our fellow-men. This we ask, through Jesus Christ our Lord.'

William Barclay was, without doubt, one of the greatest Christian communicators of our day.

A distinguished scholar, he used his learning to 'make the words of Jesus live' as much for the 'plain man' as for the student.

These daily readings, culled from his many books, are divided into texts and prayers, and display to the full Barclay's unique and compelling Christian vision.

A Question of Healing

The Reflections of a Doctor and a Priest

GARETH TUCKWELL AND DAVID FLAGG

This is a book for everybody – in the Church and outside it – who believes that there is a ministry of Christian healing, and who wants to know how it can be applied in a variety of different situations.

It is organized around a series of questions, to which Gareth Tuckwell, a doctor, and David Flagg, a priest, respond. Both have worked at the world-famous Burrswood Christian Centre for Medical and Spiritual Care in the south-east of England.

Among the subjects addressed are the importance of touch, cancer, 'pills or prayer?', the value of teamwork, healing miracles, the death of a loved one, alternative therapies, M.E., eating disorders, inner healing and living with suffering.

The authors' advice is highly practical, biblically illustrated and thoughtfully balanced. It makes the book an essential resource in a growing and thriving area where it is crucial to be discerning in one's approach.

Shaking a Fist At God

Understanding Suffering through the Book of Job

KATHARINE DELL

Shaking a Fist At God is a brilliant study of the different human responses to suffering. Although it is based upon the book of Job and written from a Christian perspective, it is packed with wisdom for believers and non-believers alike.

Job's reactions to the horrors of his situation are exceedingly human. He in angry and resentful and places the blame upon others, especially God. His friends tell Job that his suffering is punishment for sin, but he finds this inadequate. He has to conclude, stoically, that pain is the natural consequence of life in a free world.

For the Christian, there is another dimension: in the suffering of Christ on the cross God shared in our pain. His loving nature was revealed, inspiring us with hope for the future.

Never lecturing the reader, and with a colourful and entertaining reading of the Bible text, Katharine Dell establishes herself as a significant new writer on the spiritual life.